# THE CASUALTY OF CONTEMPT

## THE ALARMING RISE OF
# ANTISEMITISM
### and What Can Be Done to Stop It

By
Robert W. Ash, Brittany Bertsche, Dale Brown, Aaron David Fruh, Gerald McDermott,
David A. Meola, Bruce Pearl, Stuart J. Roth, Carrie Elise Simms, Jay Alan Sekulow,
Yisroel Stefansky, Dexter Van Zile, Joshua David Washington, Olga Meshoe
Washington, Marlene Warshawski Yahalom, Amy Zewe

FOREWORDS BY **COACH DALE BROWN,
COACH BRUCE PEARL, AND STUART J. ROTH**

GENERAL EDITOR, **AARON DAVID FRUH**
**PRESIDENT OF**
**ISRAEL TEAM ADVOCATES INTERNATIONAL**

*The Casualty of Contempt: The Alarming Rise of Antisemitism and What Can Be Done to Stop It*

Copyright © 2020 by Aaron David Fruh and Israel Team Advocates International
Published by Deep River Books
Sisters, Oregon
www.deepriverbooks.com

ISBN – 13: 9781632695628
Library of Congress Control Number: 2020925245

Printed in the USA
Cover design by Sam Noerr/Gyroscope

# CONTENTS

# FOREWORD

By
**Coach Dale Brown, Coach Bruce Pearl,
and Stuart J. Roth**

atred of the Jews has always been a great time saver, because it
enables one to form opinions without bothering to get the facts.
Time is cluttered with the wreckage of nations, communities, and
individuals who not only held contempt toward their Jewish neighbors
but allowed this abhorrence to mutate into physical acts of violence that
in many cases led to murderous animalistic rampages. The author Napoleon Hill once said, "When the dawn of intelligence shall spread over the
eastern horizon of human progress, and ignorance and superstition shall
have left their last footprints on the sands of time, it will be recorded by
the last chapter of the book of man's crimes, that his most grievous sin
was that of intolerance." He was right, of course. Over the centuries,
men and women have betrayed their very souls to create a space within
their hearts to provide asylum for antisemitism. Like the alluring sirens
in Homer's *Odyssey* that drew sailors to their deaths upon the rocky crags,
a contempt toward Jews has led to a multitude of casualties for those
who have embraced it. Because of the overwhelming number of people
in history who have been seduced into tasting the poisonous venom of
antisemitism, intolerance toward Jewish people (in my estimation) must
be the sweetest morsel ever cooked in hell. Sadly, it seems, the world

is not yet aware of the sickening side effects of embracing intolerance toward the Jews because it is still far too willing to explore the depths of its darkness. In the United States alone, according to FBI statistics, there has been a 37% rise of antisemitic incidents in the last three years. Will we follow Europe into the abyss of hatred that led its citizens to commit genocide? I pray this will not be so. This book is a warning to America concerning the treacherous rise of antisemitism in the country we hold dear. Give serious attention to the evidence the authors record. Allow their conclusions to arrest your soul with a deep soberness that leads you to courageously stand up against this growing tide of violence and contempt toward our Jewish kinsmen.

**—Coach Dale Brown**

I am honored to be a part of Israel Team's publication, *The Casualty of Contempt*. A book of this nature is not one of those "feel good" literary works you read for personal edification. It is, however, an important contribution to your understanding of why the world has historically persecuted the Jewish people. This book serves as a manifesto to counter the tragic resurgence of antisemitism in our time. The late Rabbi Jonathan Sacks once said that to find purpose and meaning in life one needs to align their passions with some good work that needs to be done for the common good of others. This book reflects the combined heartfelt passion of sixteen authors who are attempting to do the good work of righting a terrible wrong.

I was born in 1960, fifteen years after the gates of Auschwitz fell open and the world discovered the atrocities behind its walls. The most catastrophic event of our times was the Holocaust. My mother was the daughter of Jewish immigrants from a small village in Russia, where pogroms drove them from their homes. My father's father at age fourteen fled Austria, bringing his three younger siblings to America without his parents because the family only had enough money to save four lives. Both of my parents lost loved ones in the Holocaust. I remember being seated next to my parents' Jewish relatives at our family Shabbat table in Boston as a young boy. As aunts and uncles lifted the Challah bread toward heaven as the blessing was proclaimed, I noticed numbers on their arms and asked my father what the numbers meant. He explained to me that in the death camps all Jews were tattooed with serial numbers as if they were no longer human. I have never forgotten the lump that formed in my throat when I was first told about the Nazi genocide of my people.

Let me ask you a question: Throughout history, why have men fought and killed other men? Is there a common denominator? I think one reason might be a lack of tolerance for each other's differences: "I pray this way; you pray that way or not at all. My skin is this color; yours is that color. I live on this side of the river; you live on that side of the river." Instead of appreciating and embracing our differences, we are threatened by them. Racism is fueled by the refusal to understand and embrace our differences. We should recognize our differences, celebrate them, and do everything we can to live in peace.

Rabbi Sacks has declared that this refusal to embrace our differences is at the core of all racial hatred, "...if we're not Jewish, what has it (anti-semitism) got to do with us? The answer is that antisemitism is about the inability of a group to make space for difference. And because we are all different, the hate that begins with Jews never ends with Jews. It wasn't Jews alone who suffered under Hitler. It wasn't Jews alone who suffered under Stalin. It isn't Jews alone who suffer under the radical Islamists and others who deny Israel's right to exist. Antisemitism is the world's most reliable early warning sign of a major threat to freedom, humanity, and the dignity of difference. It matters to all of us. Which is why we must fight it together."

We all need to align our heartfelt passion to the good work of fighting antisemitism because antisemitism is a threat to all of humanity. This book will awaken your heart to the crucial issue of the infestation of antisemitism in our day and will inspire the boldness you will need to help shield your Jewish friends from the darkness of hate.

**—Coach Bruce Pearl**

Antisemitism is a cancer, a malignant one at that. Most of us associate it with the Holocaust, a chapter of hatred that must never be forgotten. In reality, the Holocaust was the culmination of centuries of contempt of Jews in Europe which now serves as an historical focal point in the chronicles of antisemitism.

If we fail to come to grips with what actually took place during the Holocaust, we run the risk of allowing the silence that paved the way for genocide to return. The grotesque reality of the Holocaust is that the world sat in silent indifference as Europe annihilated most of its Jewish population. Hitler and his collaborators throughout Europe waited until he was certain the nations, including America, refused the Jews no quarter or mercy—then he struck. Had the world not been indifferent toward whether the Jews survived individually or collectively, there would have been no forced expulsions into the ghettos, no cattle cars transporting Jewish souls, no death camps, and no gas chambers. It was in fact this active indifference that looked the other way when six million Jewish innocents—including one million Jewish children—were hunted down by the Nazis and shot, gassed, tortured, and starved to death. The brutality that Christian Europe exhibited toward its Jewish fellow citizens was widely known yet the world remained silent—allowing Hitler's willing executioners to unleash their rage toward the Jews, uninterrupted.

The question we must all ask ourselves is, will we personally and collectively remain silent in the present surge of antisemitism in America and throughout the world? Germany and Europe have never recovered from the moral bankruptcy that led to their crimes against the Jews. The collapse of Christianity and the resurgence of radical Islam throughout

Europe is one of the great casualties of history that was made possible by Europe's criminal contempt toward the Jewish people.

A book of this nature is long overdue. The authors share a common passion with a growing group of leaders from many disciplines that are choosing to be silent no more. As a civil rights attorney, my heart is full as I join fellow Jews and non-Jews in the pages of this book to refute and defy the growing violence toward Jewish students on college campuses, assaults against rabbis and Jewish worshipers in Synagogues, and antisemitic rhetoric fomenting across social media. My prayer is that this book serves as a wake-up call to the shocking reality that the world is reaching pre-Holocaust levels of hatred toward Jews. May there be more courageous people like you who are reading these words—willing to push back against antisemitism whenever it reveals its hideous face.

**—Stuart J. Roth**

# INTRODUCTION

by
**Aaron David Fruh**
**President of Israel Team Advocates International**

America is on the brink of following Europe in its historic normal-ization and acceptance of antisemitism. Historically, when a nation shows contempt toward the Jewish people, that nation suffers an incalculable loss. In the biblical book of Genesis chapter 12, verse 3, God speaks to Abraham and says, "I will bless those who bless you and curse those who treat you with contempt" (NLT). Interestingly, God uses two different Hebrew words for the word "curse" in this passage. The first usage is the Hebrew word, *arar*. The meaning of *arar* is "To cause to become fruitless and powerless." The second usage is the Hebrew word *kilel*. The meaning of *kilel* is "To show contempt, despise, revile, or humiliate." God is saying, "Whoever shows contempt (*kilel*) toward the Jewish people I will cause to become fruitless and powerless (*arar*)." Thus, the title of this book, *The Casualty of Contempt*. The alarming rise of antisemitism in America and around the world should be of great concern to all Americans. The fate of Jews, Israel, and the whole of the modern world hangs in the balance as a result of allowing the scourge of Jewish hatred to increase exponentially.

The nations of the earth are supernaturally connected to the Jewish people. Deuteronomy 32:8–9 says, "When the Most High gave to the nations their inheritance when He separated the children of men, He set the bounds of the peoples according to the number of the children of Israel. For Jehovah's portion is His people, Jacob is the lot of His inheritance." So, every nation on earth, whether they understand it or appreciate it, has a divine connection to Israel and the Jewish people. Therefore, to show contempt toward the Jews is to revile and despise the God of the Jews, who has chosen to identify Himself as "The God of Israel."

This book exposes the festering open wound of antisemitism and chronicles the unattended sore's insidious spread. The authors come from various fields of influence: sports, law, theology, politics, academia, journalism, and Jewish advocacy. They also represent different religious backgrounds: Judaism, Evangelicalism, Catholicism, and Anglicanism. One of the things every author has in common is a historic understanding of the roots of Jewish hatred and a passion to raise the awareness about the cancer of antisemitism before the malignant growth becomes inoperable.

In America, the growing physical violence toward and murder of Jewish people, the defacing of Jewish synagogues and cemeteries, the treacherous rise of antisemitism on both secular and Christian campuses, the constant anti-Jewish rhetoric being fomented on Twitter and YouTube, the athletes, comedians, musicians, and actors attempting to make old Jewish tropes from Medieval times a new acceptable norm, all point to the sobering fact antisemitism has transformed into something like the hideous creature in Franz Kafka's *Metamorphosis*. A kind of sickly, grotesque monster oozing with contempt. Our society has attempted to contain this vicious creature since the Holocaust, but now because of America's silent indifference, those who loathe Jews have clothed the ravenous beast of antisemitism in modern attire in an attempt to make the centuries-old deceptive myths about Jews vogue. It was German indifference to the persecution of the Jews that gave Nazi antisemites their voice, and it is American indifference to the persecution of the Jews that gives present antisemites theirs.

The Holocaust is the most horrific universal tragedy in modern times, not only for the Jews but for all of mankind. For the most part, the world has swept the Holocaust under the rug of time and history and, in some cases, denied it happened. If we don't endeavor to discover how something so blatantly inhuman could be allowed to happen in supposedly civilized Europe, then the world and the Jewish people, in particular, will experience irreparable loss because, without a sincere reckoning with history, history is bound to repeat itself. The heart cry of every author in this book is to awaken, challenge, and encourage Americans toward an awareness that the coals of antisemitism have been ignited all across our nation and around the world. From college campuses, internet sites, print publications, television, theological seminaries, and church pulpits—hatred toward Jews is becoming an acceptable norm. The pages of this book serve as a clarion call for those who desire to be informed about the growing threat antisemitism poses for all of us and what we can do collectively to prevent its continued expansion on our shores before contempt towards God's chosen people leads to a terrible casualty for our nation.

# Chapter One

# CONFRONTING THE INDIFFERENCE IN A GORILLA SUIT

**by**
**Bruce Pearl**

few years ago, I attended a Major League baseball game with my family. Near the entrance to the stadium, a man dressed in a gorilla suit held a large sign that read, "F—k the Jews! They dominate the world!" The message? Jews come from monkeys, they control the world's economy, and they must be annihilated.

As we stood in line to purchase tickets to the game, I was motionless and paralyzed. I wondered why someone would crawl inside a sweltering gorilla suit on a hot summer day to foment hatred. Hundreds of people passed by the gorilla but seemed indifferent to the message. I was born into a Jewish family, and my relatives endured this kind of vile antagonism for a long time. I wondered why no one was stopping to challenge the mocking and jeering gorilla. My protective fatherly instinct kicked in because I felt his violent message was targeting my Jewish children that stood in line with me. Here was a guy blatantly calling for another genocide of the Jews, and no one interfered. I decided to interfere. I stepped out of the long line of fans and walked towards the gorilla.

The closer I got, the deeper my resolve became to never stand idly by when someone is being treated unjustly. I wasn't filled with rage. That would have been too easy. I was motivated by righteous anger. A man was attempting to inspire violence toward my kids, and I couldn't remain silent because silent indifference towards a hateful zealot only fuels their determination. There is a law in the Torah that forbids apathetic indifference toward a person or group oppressing others. The Rabbis teach this law places a binding obligation upon us not to be silent when others are being threatened or harmed. The principle comes from Leviticus 19:16: "Do not stand idly by when your brother's blood is shed" (paraphrase). I felt burdened and obligated to confront the hate head on.

When I stood before the gorilla, something within me—a kind of deep awareness of the historical suffering of my people caused by antisemitism—rose to the surface, and with tears filling my eyes, I pointed to my heart and heard myself saying, "*Juden.*" *Juden* is the German word for Jew inscribed on the yellow stars Jews were forced to wear during the Holocaust. It was the only word I could muster. The man said nothing. Again, I pointed to my heart and said, "*Juden.*" This time I was shouting! Again, the gorilla said nothing. I had just rocked the guy's silent world with one simple word of dissent expressed with passion. Up to that point, I doubt the man had faced any objection to his threatening rhetoric. As I stared past the mask into the eyes of the man, I saw cold contempt. Again I shouted "*Juden*" and then added, "Take off your mask so we can talk face to face, and if you want, you can throw the first punch!" Was I hoping for a brawl? Maybe. The two eyes staring back at me expressed no emotion. They were filled with a kind of grey and foreboding emptiness. I realized the man behind the mask had no conscience. At that point, almost robotically, the gorilla slowly turned his back on me. There I was, a lone Jew in a sea of indifferent onlookers, facing the hairy back of an antisemitic gorilla that held a sign demanding my family's slaughter. I took his sign and broke it apart, holding the two halves in my hands as the gorilla walked away from the stadium.

In that moment, I learned two important things: An antisemite is a coward at heart who hides behind derogatory stereotypes, fabricated history, Jewish conspiracy theories, religious myths, and in this case, a gorilla costume. Secondly, I learned most people would rather remain silently indifferent to antisemitism because they think it doesn't affect them.

Let me tell you why the gorilla and all those who silently passed by without objection have it wrong, and what that can mean for us all, Jews and non-Jews alike.

I was born in 1960, fifteen years after the gates of Auschwitz fell open and the world discovered the atrocities behind its walls. Jewish people have vowed this will never happen again . . . to anyone.

As a Jewish man, I have lived with antisemitism my whole life, and I have seen its ugly face many times. So has my family, for many generations. My surname, Pearl, was originally Pearlmutter. The name has its roots in economic antisemitism. Due to the laws that prevented Jews from entering into skilled professions during medieval times and beyond, Jews were forced into trading in pearls, diamonds, gold, and silver, then compelled to change their surnames to match their occupations. Many of the Jewish surnames today come from their professions as jewelers through the centuries: Silverstein, Goldberg, Goldschmidt, Green (the color of emeralds), Shafire (Yiddish for sapphire), and yes, Pearlmutter, which means "mother of pearl."

One of the more insulting stereotypes, promoted by the person in the gorilla suit, is that the Jewish people are all rich and control the world's monetary system. My Jewish upbringing did not match this false narrative.

I grew up in a Boston middle-class neighborhood on the third floor of a three-flat apartment building. My father, Bernie Pearl, taught me the work ethic I have today. He was a traveling salesman and worked long, hard hours to support our family. My mother, Barbara, worked full-time as a secretary for the Muscular Dystrophy Association. When my dad took our family for supper at Burger King every once and awhile on Sunday evenings, it was a special treat. So, our family was certainly not rich. My mother is now eighty-four years of age and recently visited Brandy and me in Auburn, Alabama. One morning as she sat on our back porch looking out over the lake, I noticed tears running down her cheeks.

My mother was the daughter of Jewish immigrants from a small village in Russia, where pogroms drove them from their homes. She lost relatives and loved ones in the Holocaust. Each teardrop flowing down my mother's beautiful cheeks was filled with history and pain. She looked at me with those reassuring motherly Jewish eyes and said, "Your father and I were the first in our family to own a single-family home, and to see how God has blessed you with this home in this beautiful setting brings me joy." I had broken free from the shackles of antisemitism, and she was grateful.

Have I faced difficulties along the way as a Division 1 Jewish basketball coach? Sure. When my team, the Auburn Tigers, reached the Final Four of the national championship in 2019, it was a triumph on so many levels for the players, the coaching staff, and the university. As I celebrated with the Auburn family I have come to love, there was a little voice telling me not to forget: I didn't become one of five Jewish basketball coaches in history to reach the Final Four on my own. I was standing on the shoulders of my Jewish ancestors who suffered dishonor and prejudice in order to give me a shot in life. I also knew I was standing on the shoulders of the universities that had given a Jewish man the chance to coach basketball at their schools. I am truly grateful for the Universities of Southern Indiana, Wisconsin Milwaukee, and Tennessee, and Auburn University.

One set of those shoulders belonged to my grandfather, Jack Pearlmutter, who we affectionately called "Papa Jack." My paternal grandparents emigrated from Europe in 1909. They settled in Mattapan, Boston, a thriving Jewish community of new immigrants mainly from Poland and Russia. The neighborhoods were dotted with dilapidated triple-decker Victorians that lined a three-mile stretch of Blue Hill Avenue. The Jews of Mattapan became known as "The Blue Hill Avenue Jews." Though a poor Jewish community (some have called it a slum), the Blue Hill Avenue Jews would build twenty-five synagogues, the original Beth Israel Hospital, and the Home for Destitute Jewish Children. Because of its commitment to religious education, Mattapan would eventually define standards for Jewish education and provide training for Hebrew teachers across America. Blue Hill Avenue Jews were the first American Jews to adopt Zionism, the hope of one day returning to the land of Israel. I'm proud to be a descendant of this flourishing hamlet of poor Jews.

Papa Jack was a plumber and had fingers the size of thumbs. I remember sitting at my grandmother Nana's kitchen table when Papa would come home from a long day's work. He would stand over the sink and scrub the black pipe grease from his hands with a steel wool brush. Papa and Nana lived in a small duplex, and I can assure you, controlling the world's finances was not something that crossed their minds. I would like to think that if my frugal Papa Jack was actually in charge of the American economy, we wouldn't be over twenty trillion in debt.

Papa Jack and Nana Rose lived simply and retained the deep Jewish values from the old country. They kept kosher and spoke Yiddish more than English in their home. On Friday evenings and Saturdays, Papa would bring me with him to shul. The more sophisticated and wealthy Jewish men at shul showed my papa utmost regard. During the week Papa repaired pipes, installed toilets and faucets, but on the Sabbath at shul, Papa stood shoulder to shoulder with doctors and lawyers as an equal.

The Torah teaches as much about how we are to treat our neighbors with kindness and honor as it does about how we are to respect and love God. Seeing these men treat my papa as an equal taught me to respect every person I meet without prejudice. I think that is one reason why I have always been so passionate about fighting inequality. It says in the Torah that God did not choose Israel because she was a great and powerful nation. He set His love on her because she was small and insignificant (Deuteronomy 7:7, paraphrase). It also says God shows no partiality toward anyone (Deuteronomy 10:17, paraphrase).

During Israel's Six-Day War in 1967, I saw my Papa Jack crying as he watched the evening news. He told me about Israel and how she was under attack. Normally, Papa would fall asleep in his easy chair, but on this night, he was wide awake. He hesitated closing his eyes because he feared Israel would not exist when he woke up. As I look back on that night, I realize the deep impression my papa's tears for Israel left on my memory. I realized at the young age of seven—twenty-two years after the Holocaust—how vulnerable Israel was. I discovered in that moment that I as a Jew am somehow intricately and spiritually connected to the land of Israel. When I hear the violent rhetoric today about Israel's annihilation, my thoughts go back to 1967, sitting at Papa Jack's feet in that little duplex in Mattapan on Greendale Road just off of Blue Hill Avenue.

Israel has faced a continual existential threat from her early beginnings, and the drumbeat for her destruction is getting louder. I think perhaps my love for Israel has intrigued and inspired my wife Brandy and my children Jacqui, Steven, Leah, and Michael to connect to the land and cherish their Hebraic roots and Jewish identity. Each of my children over the last few years has had a Star of David, Hebrew letters, or scripture tattooed on their arms or other areas of their bodies. My conservative Jewish upbringing forbids tattoos, but there is a kindred solidarity with my children drawing me to do the same. It's a reminder to me that they escaped the numbers the Nazis tattooed on the arms of Jews in the death camps. It is a declaration of courage to stand with the Jewish people both past and present who have been persecuted.

I was honored to coach the US men's squad in the 18th Maccabiah Games in Israel in 2009. These games attract Jewish athletes from around the world to compete in a multisport event. It is widely known as "The Jewish Olympics." Of course, our American team of young Jewish athletes was there to play basketball—we would win the gold medal—but I also saw these games as a way to connect my players to Israel and to their Jewish identity. My wife, Brandy, videoed our team's journey through Israel. My daughter Jacqui was the team manager. Jacqui served the team, keeping them hydrated during the games and even doing their laundry. I had the unique privilege of coaching my son Steven, who received a gold medal in the tournament. My parents, Bernie and Barbara, traveled with the team as well and even got to see a forest of trees they had helped plant years before. Our team attended temple on Shabbat, ate in Jewish restaurants, prayed at the Western Wall, and toured the country. This was my first trip to Israel, and when I set foot on the land—maybe it was the Zionism inspired in me from the Blue Hill Avenue Jews of Mattapan—I knelt down and kissed the earth.

Today, Israel once again stands at the crossroads as the nations rage against her and demand she relinquish more land for peace. On a recent trip to Israel, Brandy, who has a profound love for Israel and the Jewish people, and I were a part of a delegation sponsored by our friend Heather Johnston of JH Israel and the United States Israel Education Association (USIEA). We visited an Israeli hospital in the Golan Heights where Israeli doctors and nurses administer lifesaving medical treatment to refugees from Syria, a country that has vowed to destroy Israel. Syria has partnered with Iran in order to commit mass genocide of the Jews. The murderous regime, Iran, is financing this terrorist operation. Sadly, within our own Congress there are voices calling for Israel's destruction.

During this same trip, we visited Israeli factories in Judea and Samaria in the Jordan Valley, an area also known as the West Bank. I was amazed to talk to Palestinian and Israeli employees working side by side without malice. The Peace to Prosperity plan that is unfolding today was already in the works. The Palestinians were happy to work for Jewish companies that treated them with dignity. They appreciated the healthcare benefits and the excellent income and have made it known they would rather live under the Israeli government than the Palestinian Authority. We shared an evening meal with Sheikh Ashraf Al-Jabari, a Palestinian business leader at odds with the warmongering culture of death inspired by Hamas and the Palestinian Authority. Leaders like Al-Jabari are desirous of a lasting peace and partnership with Israel so that the Palestinian people who long for a better life can begin to prosper. They agree with what former Prime Minister of Israel Golda Meir once said, "Peace will come when Arabs love their children more than they hate us."

Remarkably, the Boycott, Divestment, Sanctions (BDS) movement, an antisemitic group attempting to cripple Israel's economy, is committed to closing Israeli companies that employ Palestinian workers. Why? The optic of happy Palestinians working in harmony next to their Israeli neighbors does not fit the BDS anti-Israel narrative. Soda Stream is a good example. The company intentionally built its factory in Judea and Samaria in order to employ over five hundred Palestinians. In many cases, Palestinians were promoted to manage their fellow Jewish employees. The BDS movement, ideologically devoted only to its false narrative about Israel and not to the needs of the Palestinians, forced the company out of the West Bank, hurting five hundred Palestinian employees. The BDS movement could not embrace the idea of Jews and Palestinians working together in peace for prosperity.

The sad truth is Palestinian leadership has been allotted billions upon billions of dollars over the years in foreign aid in order to provide an excellent quality of life for their people. This money could have easily provided healthcare, schools, parks, decent housing, and roads. Instead, much of the financial aid has gone into the pockets of Palestinian leaders, making billionaires of several. The money has been used to reward terrorists who murder Jewish citizens, build terrorist tunnels into Israel, and build rockets to fire into southern Israel. It saddens me that the suffering of the Palestinian people created by their own leaders is being used to turn world opinion against Israel. If the Palestinian people should begin to prosper, it would destroy the argument that Israel is an oppressive regime. Their political leaders care more about hating Jews than caring for their own citizens.

As a Jew, I am a sworn enemy of the Palestinian leadership that rejects the Jewish right of existence and self-determination in the land of Israel. Some of the same leaders call for the annihilation of every Jew in every corner of the earth. Tell me, how can there be peace between two sides in a conflict when one side wants the other side dead? Over the centuries, Jews have been driven from one country to another, and Israel is a place of refuge for Jews fleeing antisemitism. The Jews literally have nowhere else to run. Golda Meir once said, "The Egyptians could run to Egypt, the Syrians into Syria. The only place we (Israelis) could run was into the sea." I and many other Jews and Christians alike desire to see the Palestinian people enjoy a better quality of life, and we are hopeful that a peace through prosperity plan will gain traction.

The antisemitism I describe hurts more than just Jews. It hurts all people, everywhere. My papa, Jack Pearlmutter, died when I was thirteen. I hadn't been to many funerals, but I remember on the way to the cemetery seeing the motorcade that seemed to go on forever. At a Jewish graveside service after the rabbi prays the Kaddish and the casket is lowered into the earth, family members and friends file by the open grave. The first person in the procession picks up a shovel of dirt and throws it down on the casket. They hand the shovel to the next person in line, who does the same. I witnessed dozens and dozens of African American men and women filing past, embracing the shovel and tossing dirt over Papa's coffin. Afterward, each one came up to my nana and thanked her. My grandparents owned an apartment building in Roxbury, a predominately poor black neighborhood, and when their tenants fell on hard times and could not pay their rent, my papa would forgive their payments. I never really knew this until Papa's funeral. I remember someone once questioning Papa about why he could own an apartment building and yet still lived in a small duplex, and Papa said, "We can afford to have less so that others can have a decent roof over their heads. Besides, if I don't help them, they have nowhere else to go." For him, helping the poor was a mitzvah, fulfilling a command-ment to do good to one's neighbor. He kept his acts of mercy quiet, and the truth came out only after he was gone.

As I look back now, I realize Papa felt a kindred bond with his Afri-can American friends because of the hardships both Jews and African Americans have had to endure. My parents and grandparents taught me the great truth of valuing every person without showing favoritism.

One of the things that inspires and challenges me is that we are all brothers and sisters. We are all part of the human family. Jesus was born a Jew, and He died a Jew. That makes me a brother to my Christian brothers and sisters. Abraham had two sons: Isaac and Ismael. That means I, as a Jew, am connected to my Arab brothers and sisters. All of us in the human family have more in common than we realize. We should celebrate our commonality. We should never tolerate racism or antisemitism of any kind. As a basketball coach, I ingrain into my players the idea that when we work together as a team, not only is the entire team successful but every individual on the team is successful as well. There is so much more good in this world than there is evil, and we need to celebrate that good. But, at the same time, we need to call out the evil of antisemitism and racism whenever and wherever we see it. I have always seen myself as a uniter, not a divider. Certainly, somehow in this world, we can learn how to appreciate our differences and love one another.

The name given to me at my bris on the eighth day of my life was Mordechai. Mordechai was the Jewish uncle of Queen Esther in the Bible. Mordechai and Esther were instrumental in staying the hand of the antisemite, Haman, who sought to ethnically cleanse the world of all of its Jews. I have always felt fighting injustice toward my people was a burden God imparted to me as a young Jewish kid growing up in Boston. As a Mordechai in my generation, I feel responsible to push back against Jewish hatred whenever it raises its head.

Why? Because antisemitism is an early warning sign that hatred and bigotry are on the rise—not just toward Jews but toward everyone. The alarming rise of violent and hateful antisemitism in our world today, the beliefs that gave that man in the gorilla suit permission to proclaim his hatred, is contagious.

According to the Anti-Defamation League, in the last year alone, America has experienced a 56 percent increase in violent acts against Jews. Every eighty-three seconds, a new antisemitic message is posted on social media. More than half of religious hate crimes in America are against Jews. Three-fourths of Jewish students on American college campuses have witnessed antisemitic acts on their campuses.

In Europe, antisemitism is rising to the levels of 1930s Germany. Jews are fleeing France in record numbers because of growing violence against them. The desecration of synagogues and Jewish cemeteries is now commonplace throughout Europe. Here in America, it is becoming the norm for sports figures, musicians, and Hollywood stars to tweet antisemitic tropes. Radical Islamists the world over are calling for the ethnic cleansing of all Jews in the land of Israel. Anti-Israel protesters are chanting, "From the river [the Jordan River] to the sea [the Mediterranean] Palestine will be free." The message: "We will ethnically cleanse Israel of all of its Jews." In the Holy name of the God of Abraham, Isaac, and Jacob, please tell me where my Jewish brothers and sisters can live in safety?

But that's just a Jewish problem, right? Rabbi Jonathan Sacks wrote,

> . . . if we're not Jewish, what has it got to do with us? The answer is that antisemitism is about the inability of a group to make space for difference. And because we are all different, the hate that begins with Jews never ends with Jews. It wasn't Jews alone who suffered under Hitler. It wasn't Jews alone who suffered under Stalin. It isn't Jews alone who suffer under the radical Islamists and others who deny Israel's right to exist. Antisemitism is the world's most reliable early warning sign of a major threat to freedom, humanity, and the dignity of difference. It matters to all of us. Which is why we must fight it together.[1]

Actor and poet Géza Röhrig said, "It wasn't God who rounded up the Jews and the Gypsies and the Soviet POWs and the gays and the perfectly

---

[1] Rabbi Jonathan Saks, "The Mutation of Antisemitism," April 17, 2019, https://rabbisacks.org

German mental patients and the perfectly German midgets and slaughtered them. We did it. The human family did it." I think what he was saying was, if ordinary German citizens allowed hatred to go unchecked to the point of this kind of mass genocide toward people who were different, it could happen again.

If we in the human family do not challenge antisemitism, we become an accessory to its evil. Like the people who passed by the hostile man in the gorilla costume without challenging him, indifference is compliance.

In her book *One, by One, by One*, about facing the truth of the Holocaust, Pulitzer Prize-winning author Judith Miller writes, ". . . before the Holocaust was a national and international catastrophe, it was a family tragedy, and individual loss. History books and education are important. But my memory of a single infant's leather shoe encased in glass at Yad Vashem in Jerusalem is as powerful. Abstraction is memory's most ardent enemy. It kills because it encourages distance, and often indifference. We must remind ourselves that the Holocaust was not six million. It was one, plus one, plus one. . . . Only in understanding that civilized people must defend the one, by one, by one . . . can the Holocaust, the incomprehensible, be given meaning."

I want to do all I can to keep the memory of the victims of the Holocaust alive. Perhaps the memory of their sacrifice and suffering will prevent another genocide somewhere in the world. Maybe it will also awaken the world to the ongoing persecution of the Jewish people. In his speech during the dedication ceremony of the Holocaust museum in Jerusalem, Holocaust survivor Elie Wiesel said, "And so we go through the museum and what should we do? Weep? No. My good friends, we never try to tell the tale to make people weep. It's too easy. We didn't want pity. If we decided to tell the tale, it is because we wanted the world to be a better world—just a better world, and learn, and remember." For Wiesel, keeping the memory of the Holocaust alive was a way to fight injustice toward any person. When Elie Wiesel gave his acceptance speech upon winning the Nobel Peace Prize in 1986, he stated,

> . . . I swore never to be silent when and wherever human beings endure suffering and humiliation. We must always take sides. Brutality helps the oppressor, never the victim. Silence encourages the tormentor, never the tormented. Sometimes we must interfere. When human lives are endangered, when human dignity is in jeopardy, national borders and sensitivities become irrelevant. Whenever men and women are persecuted because of their race, religion or political views, that must—at that moment—become the center of the universe.

As I said earlier, indifference to another person's suffering—like the crowds that allowed the man in the gorilla suit to incite violence unchallenged—is actually compliance. As long as there is inequality in elementary and secondary education, we cannot keep silent. As long as there is racial profiling in our criminal justice system, we must not be silent. All expressions of racism should receive pushback. We cannot shrink back in silence as antisemitism grows ever more vocal and violent. It's time we choose to interfere rather than pass by the man in the gorilla suit.

I think I inherited the surname Pearlmutter—mother of pearl—for a reason. Mother of pearl is the secretion an oyster wraps around an irritating grain of sand that is wounding its flesh, forming the costly pearl. My grandparents, my parents, my wife, children, grandchildren, and so many others, we are creating pearls—something good and decent and beautiful—out of suffering. May the Jewish people, bound by suffering to so many other people at the margins all across the world, have the power to stand up together, and break in half the signs that would seek to diminish and destroy us.

## ABOUT THE AUTHOR

Bruce Pearl is the head men's basketball coach for the Auburn Tigers at Auburn University. Coach Pearl also coached at Tennessee, Milwaukee, and Southern Indiana. Coach Pearl led Indiana to a Division II National Championship and was named the National Association of Basketball Division II coach of the year in 1995. Coach Pearl was named coach of the year by Sporting News in 2006 and was awarded the Rupp Cup in 2008. He also served as the head coach for the Maccabi USA men's basketball team in the 2009 Maccabi Games in Tel Aviv, Israel, where he led the US to win the gold medal. In 2019, Coach Pearl led Auburn to the Final Four in the NCAA championship. He is one of five Jewish coaches in history to reach the Final Four. Coach Pearl is a vocal supporter of Israel and the Jewish people and is a leader in the fight against antisemitism.

*Chapter Two*

# THE RAILROAD TIE IN AUSCHWITZ THAT CHANGED MY LIFE

### by
### Dale Brown

I have traveled to eighty-seven countries in our world, but no international experience affected me so emotionally, markedly, even severely as the one to Krakow, Poland. The memory is etched so deeply in my conscience; it seems as though it were yesterday, even though it happened over thirty years ago. As my wife Vonnie and I enjoyed the culture of Krakow, there was a stirring inside of me to venture out about an hour's drive from the city to a place I had researched and thought about for many years. On a sun-drenched morning, Vonnie and I rented a vehicle and headed out to the countryside. Though the sky was a stunning blue, my mood was somber at best. It was as if a paintbrush were covering the brilliantly colored sun-drenched landscape with a kind of melancholic grey with every mile of our journey to the scene of the world's greatest crime. You see, just outside of Krakow—a city known for its museums, universities, and literature—stands the largest of the Nazi's death camps, Auschwitz, and this dreaded place was our destination. As the road lengthened before us, my heart began to melt like wax because I sensed as if I were driving to the edge of the abyss itself. And now looking back, I realize my perceptions were accurate.

Gazing out the window as I drove, I imagined the far-off whistle of a train locomotive and the monotonous clickity-clack of steel wheels against iron tracks echoing and ricocheting off the wooden beams between the rails. The trees, like great walls lining both sides of the train tracks toward the crematoriums, stood straight and upright as if they were witnesses to the Nazi crime of genocide. As we drove, I thought of the survivors of Auschwitz who could never hear the innocent and mystical whistle of a locomotive again without that same sound bringing back the wretched memory of their fear-filled transports to uncertainty—cars normally used for cattle now moving Jewish human flesh compacted so tightly by the ever-efficient diabolical Nazis that little room was left for water or air. Coffins for the dead have more space. Pushed and crammed into the cars by willing Aryan soldiers—the first seed of Germany's thousand-year Reich—and in many cases forced onto the trains by neighbors and acquaintances from their countries of origin, glad to dispose of what they called "Jewish vermin." By the time the transports made it to Auschwitz, the stench of human excrement and urine was unbearable for those who had survived the trip without suffocating from the low volume of oxygen—a consequence that many fell prey to.

As we traveled alongside the tracks to the death camp, I wondered why the allied forces, being well aware of the persecution and murder of the Jews in places like Treblinka, Auschwitz-Birkenau, Dachau, Buchenwald, Ravensbruck, Bergen-Belsen, and others, didn't bomb the railroad tracks and at least slow the Nazi well-oiled program of Jewish extermination.

When we arrived at Auschwitz and noticed the tracks ended there— a sight that for me confirmed the precision of the Germans' murderous intentions—I thought of the hundreds of thousands of Jewish men, women, and children who came down the ramps from those trains— some herded like sheep to the slaughter immediately into the gas chambers where they would be asphyxiated until dead by Ziklong B gas, then carried into the crematoriums, where the smoke carried the ashes of the innocent into the atmosphere to be driven by the winds and later descend upon the surrounding countryside. They say the towns near the death camps were covered in human ash so thick it appeared as if it were constantly winter. And yet, the townspeople—when the frenetic killing spree of their beloved Fuhrer and his willing executioners finally ended—claimed they had no clue what was happening behind the walls and the barbed wire and the tall smokestacks that never ceased coughing up the ashes of the dead.

Those that were not sent to the crematoriums were led to the workers' sections of the camp, where they would become slave laborers and quite likely die of starvation and exhaustion or be shot, hung, or tortured to death for any number of minor offenses—like stealing a piece of bread. Many in Auschwitz perished under the surgical knife of the monster and sociopath known as the Angel of Death, Dr. Josef Mengele, who performed grotesque experiments on live Jewish subjects without the aid of morphine.

As I walked through the entrance of Auschwitz, under the now-famous iron gate, which carries the German words *Arbeit Macht Frei* ("Work Sets you Free"), a kind of eerie and cold desolation arrested my soul—a feeling I have never forgotten. I thought of Holocaust survivor Elie Wiesel's description in his book, *Night*, of his first night in Auschwitz soon after he and his father had come down the ramps from the train:

> Not far from us flames, huge flames were rising from a ditch. Something was being burned there. A truck drew close and unloaded its hold: small children. Babies! Yes, I did see this with my own eyes . . . children thrown into the flames. . . . I pinched myself. Was I still alive? Was I awake? How was it possible that men, women, and children were being burned and that the world kept silent?[2]

---

[2] Elie Wiesel, *Night* (New York; Hill and Wang, 1972, 1985), 32, 34.

As Vonnie and I entered the Auschwitz museum and looked upon the remnants of man's inhumanity to man—mounds of shoes, luggage, eyeglasses, human hair shaved from the dead (tons of Jewish hair was sent to textile companies for the production of chair cushions, mattresses, and clothing for Germans), children's clothes and dolls—all kinds of emotions began reverberating through my entire being. Tremendous anger, dread, confusion, and frustration worked in unison, tying my stomach in knots to the point I felt I needed to vomit. And then the tears started flowing down my cheeks. Somewhere in the background, I could hear a whispering voice muttering over and over again, "How in the hell was this possible?" Again and again, I heard the subtle voice, "How in the hell was this possible?" The voice sounded pained, filled with desperation and angst—waiting for an answer that did not come. I looked around, wondering if others heard what I was hearing. I supposed the voice echoing off the walls of Auschwitz was someone in the museum overcome and undone by what they were seeing until it finally dawned on me that the voice was my own—crying out just under my breath, "How in the hell was this possible?"

Immediately I turned to Vonnie and said, "I cannot finish the tour right now. I have to go outside and get some fresh air."

I remember walking down a little stone trail, feeling sick and faint as I went. With each step, almost rhythmically came the words again and again, "How in the hell could this happen?" I began to search my mind for the answer. How could this happen in one of the most sophisticated cultures on earth? A culture that gave us Handel, Beethoven, Bach, and great theologians and poets? How could a cultured people systematically and bestially—without common human feeling or regard for their fellow man—carry out such a heinous crime? Again, with rising dread the question sprang from my vocal cords, "How in the hell could this happen?" The feeling of nausea began running through my veins. Closing my eyes, I reached out toward a nearby railroad tie that had been positioned vertically in the earth—like a fence post. I rested my hand there for a moment and looked up into the sky above Auschwitz, feeling the warmth of the sun on my tear-stained face. As I moved to pull my hand away, I realized my palm had been stretched across a plaque attached to the post. There on that roughly hewn railroad tie, I found the answer to the question I so desperately needed, for written on the plaque beneath my sweat-covered hand were these words:

"The road to Auschwitz was built by hate, but paved with indifference."

Ian Kershaw

When I read those words, I realized Hitler could never have acted alone in carrying out his hatred to such a cataclysmic end as the Final Solution to exterminate European Jewry. Nor could he have accomplished it with only the soldiers under his command. What Hitler needed were multitudes of German and European citizens—mostly baptized Christians—who would be indifferent to the slaughter of the Jews to such a degree they would collaborate with the Nazis in rounding up their Jewish neighbors. For multitudes of Europeans, indifference wasn't just a matter of turning a blind eye toward the slaughter of Jews. It was a partnership with evil. They suppressed human empathy while knowingly cosigning the death certificates of Jews every time they pointed them out—willingly and in many cases gleefully—to the inquiring SS. By the time the killing stopped, in Auschwitz alone over one million one hundred thousand Jews had perished. In all, over six million Jewish people were led to their deaths with the assistance of non-military European citizens who attended church on Sunday mornings while somehow remaining indifferent to their role as accessories to mass murder. This is how the Holocaust could happen.

It is a matter of history that when the Supreme Allied Commander of the Allied Expeditionary Force, General Dwight Eisenhower, found the few remaining victims of the death camps—too weak to escape the terror of their prison upon their liberation—ordered all possible photographs to be taken, and ordered the German people from surrounding villages be brought to the camps to witness the horror of what happened and to bury the dead. He gave his reason: "Get it all on record now—get the films—get the witnesses—because somewhere down the road of history some bastard will get up and say this never happened!"

Now, more than ever, with Iran, among others, claiming the Holocaust to be a total myth, it is imperative that we speak up and make sure the world never forgets this horrendous slaughter of millions of Jews. The courage and wisdom in these words from Martin Luther King become more clear with each passing day: "In these days of worldwide confusion; there is a dire need for men and women who will courageously do battle for the truth."

To say the Holocaust did not occur is far beyond insanity, and to allow the fools to totally display their sickness through antisemitism reminds me of Danish philosopher Søren Kierkegaard's statement, "There are two ways to be fooled. One is to believe what isn't truth; the other is to refuse to believe what is true."[3] Evil is only able to exist because of total apathy. Ian Kershaw made that clear in his powerful statement, "The road to Auschwitz was built by hatred but paved with indifference."

Edmund Burke, an eighteenth-century English statesman, alerted us those many centuries ago when he said, "The only thing necessary for the triumph of evil is for good men to do nothing. Nobody makes a greater mistake than he who did nothing because he could only do a little." A perfect example of this would be a prominent German pastor, Martin Niemöller, as he would famously confess after the war that he did not speak out on behalf of the Jews when the Nazis arrested them. His scorn and lack of empathy for the Jews was clear. He finally stated, "Our guilt as Christians was much greater than the guilt of the Nazis because we knew what was right. Six million Jews were cold-bloodily murdered in our midst and in our name." By coming to terms with his past and

---

[3] Sir Ian Kershaw, *Popular Opinion and Political Dissent in the Third Reich* (Bavaria, 1933-45, 1983) 277

dedicating his later life to the service of justice, peace, and love for one's neighbors, he should inspire all of us to never let evil flourish. Dr. Harry Edwards, civil rights icon, said, "Silence is evil's greatest ally."

Elie Wiesel, a survivor of the Holocaust and winner of the Nobel Peace Prize, said, "We must always take sides. Neutrality helps the oppressor, never the victim. Silence encourages the tormentor, never the tormented. There may be times when we are powerless to prevent injustice, but there must never be a time we fail to protest." Albert Einstein said, "It is not the evil people I worry about, but it is all the good people that do nothing about the evil people." We all must have the courage and energy to speak up about the evil and a plan to crush it. Evil is relentless, but it can be crushed by courage and taking immediate and massive action to strangle it. It is impossible to compromise with evil because from the beginning of mankind whenever good compromised with evil, evil always won. Silence and apathy all through history have been the catalyst to allow sick and deranged cowards to spew their hatred. Like a school bully, they are wimps, and when confronted, they are spineless.

Famous author Napoleon Hill said, "When the dawn of intelligence shall spread over the eastern horizon of human progress, and ignorance and superstition shall have left their last footprints on the sands of time, it will be recorded by the last chapter of the book of man's crimes, that his most grievous sin was that of intolerance." Only through an inner spiritual transformation do we gain the strength and courage to fight vigorously the evils of the world. Time is cluttered with the wreckage of communities that surrendered to hatred and violence. For the salvation of mankind, we must follow another way; it is called courage. Courage sustains itself in the face of difficulty and finds the strength to persevere boldly to face evil, danger, threats, fear, intimidation, and uncertainty. Multitalented Maya Angelo described courage perfectly when she profoundly stated, "Courage is the most important of all the virtues because without courage, you can't practice any other virtue consistently."

All through the history of the world, just a few courageous and committed people brought about monumental change for the goodness of mankind by their actions. When brave and committed people make a strong stand for what is right, the spines of others are stiffened to destroy evil.

Now, what will you do to make a difference in the world? Silence, apathy, complacency, and fear are the greatest contributors to evil. Fear will paralyze you, but the boldness of faith will empower you to heights unimaginable.

We can all be divided into three groups, those who watch things happen (Silence), those who wonder what happened (Silence), and those who refuse to remain (Silent) and make things happen. None of us should ever feel, "What can little old me do?"—because that is a very lame excuse to do nothing. If you have that urge to be (Silent), think of what well-respected Charles Krauthammer said: "You're betraying your whole life if you don't say what you think." Do not remain (Silent), because in doing so you contribute to wicked and diabolic acts. We must be the change we wish to see, and that can only be done by taking immediate and massive action!

Antisemitism is tragically experiencing a rebirth, and we are now seeing it fomented in the same vitriolic rhetoric used in pre-Holocaust Germany. In the United States, FBI statistics show a 37 percent rise in antisemitic incidents in just the last three years. Shall we follow the citizens of Europe who were indifferent to antisemitism? Elie Wiesel said,

> Indifference to me, is the epitome of all evil. . . . The opposite of love is not hate, it's indifference. The opposite of beauty is not ugliness, it's indifference. The opposite of faith is not heresy, it's indifference. And the opposite of life is not death, but indifference between life and death. . . . To remain silent and indifferent is the greatest sin of all. . . . The greatest evil in the world is not anger or hatred, but indifference.

When we see evil and injustice and do nothing, we become accessories to the evil action. My experience in a courtyard in Auschwitz leaning my hand against a roughly hewn railroad tie taught me that life lesson, and I pray to God I never forget it.

## ABOUT THE AUTHOR

Coach Brown served as the head men's basketball coach of the LSU Tigers for twenty-five years. On nine occasions Coach Brown was selected as the SEC Coach of the Year or runner-up Coach of the Year. He was also chosen two times as the National College Basketball Coach of the Year. He is a member of the National Coaches Hall of Fame and selected by Bleacher Report as one of the fifty greatest coaches in college basketball history. Coach Brown is one of only seven coaches in SEC history to have led their teams to two Final Four playoffs or more. Coach Brown and Coach Rupp of Kentucky are the only SEC coaches in history to have seventeen non-losing seasons. Coach Brown was second only to Coach Rupp in winning the most SEC regular season games in history.

*Chapter Three*

# A MILLENNIAL CONFRONTS CHRISTIAN ANTISEMITISM

**by**
**Brittany Bertsche**

"Jewish studies? Why are you studying that?" If I had a dollar for every time a fellow undergraduate student asked me those questions, I would have quite a few dollars. While my choice of program may have confused my fellow students, I could not imagine studying anything else. The Lord began molding my heart for the Jewish people at a young age, when my grandmother gifted me a copy of *The Diary of a Young Girl.* Anne Frank's story captivated me, and I decided to learn all I could about the Holocaust and the Jewish people. Eventually, the Lord impressed it upon my heart to attend a Bible school with a Jewish studies program. Four years and five trips to Israel later, I live here in Israel, working on my master's degree in Holocaust studies, pursuing God's calling.

My undergraduate studies changed my life. My love for the Jewish people only grew stronger as I learned more about Judaism, Jewish history, and Jewish culture. My own faith was enriched by discovering the deep Jewish roots of Christianity—roots like the Jewishness of the

Bible, Messianic prophecy, and the role of the Jewish people in God's plan for salvation. My faith also deepened as I learned more about God's faithful love to the Jewish people. If God keeps His promises to the Jewish people, surely He will keep His promises to me! My studies also revealed an aspect of church history I was previously unaware of. For centuries, the church perpetuated and was complicit in antisemitism in varying degrees, but this history is all but missing from the church's collective memory today. As Catholic priest Edward H. Flannery poignantly explains in his book *The Anguish of the Jews,*

> The vast majority of Christians, even well educated, are all but totally ignorant of what happened to Jews in history and of the culpable involvement of the Church. Jews on the other hand are by and large acutely aware of this page of history if for no other reason than that it is so extensively and intimately intermingled with the history of the Jews and Judaism.[4]

Unfortunately, Flannery's words still ring true today: most Christians have no knowledge about the history of Christian antisemitism, but the Jewish people have not forgotten. I will never forget the first time I heard a Jewish person describe the pain the church caused her people. I had just completed my first semester of my Jewish studies program, and had learned in-depth the history of Christian antisemitism. While on an intensive educational ten-day trip to Israel with a Christian group, we listened to a lecture by an Orthodox Jewish woman in which she explained that Jews feel uncomfortable around Christians because of our tumultuous shared history. Hearing her pain, and the resulting aversion to Jesus the Messiah, broke my heart.

The Christian antisemitism that so damaged Jewish-Christian relations is still alive in the church today. I witnessed it firsthand in November

---

[4] Edward H. Flannery, *The Anguish of the Jews: Twenty-Three Centuries of Antisemitism* (New York: Paulist Press, 1999), 1.

2018, at the Christ at the Checkpoint conference in Oklahoma City. The conference, sponsored by the Palestinian Bethlehem Bible College in the West Bank and staffed by the United Methodist Church Foundation in Oklahoma, is marketed as an opportunity to "address the injustices that have taken place in the ongoing conflict between Israel and Palestine," while promoting "courageous love for Palestinian Arabs and Israeli Jews alike." And although their website explicitly states the conference leaders "do not condemn the Jewish people" and "reject any forms of anti-Semitism," the reality was far different.[5] In reality, the conference speakers spouted the same anti-Jewish theology peddled by the church for centuries.

Even though, for example, speakers denied subscribing to replacement theology (the belief that the church has replaced Israel in God's plan), they spent a good deal of time explaining why the church is now, essentially, Israel. In his morning devotions, Dr. Gary Burge explained how the New Testament teaches that the promises made to Abraham were inherited by Christ and have been expanded to the church. Therefore, the Jewish people no longer have any justifiable claim to the land of Israel, or to being God's chosen people. Stephen Sizer, a former vicar in the Anglican Church in England, and infamous for his antisemitic Facebook and blog posts,[6] said that with the expansion of the promises, "He [God] has redefined Israel."

Christian triumphalism—the idea that Christianity has wholly superseded Judaism, as Augustine believed[7]—was prevalent at the conference

---

[5] "About Christ at the Checkpoint," accessed October 5, 2020, https://christatthe-checkpoint.bethbc.edu/about-christ-at-the-checkpoint/.

[6] Brent Scher, "Pro-BDS Christian Conference to Feature Man Who Blamed Israel for 9/11," accessed October 4, 2020, https://freebeacon.com/issues/pro-bds-christian-conference-to-feature-man-who-blamed-israel-for-9-11/.

[7] David Turner, "Foundations of Antisemitism: Augustine and Christian Triumphalism," accessed October 5, 2020, https://www.jpost.com/blogs/the-jewish-problem---from-anti-judaism-to-anti-semitism/foundations-of-antisemitism-augustine-and-christian-triumphalism-365442.

as well. Rev. Bob Roberts Jr., a pastor from Keller, Texas, said in his Tuesday morning lecture that Christians "need to return to the core of the centrality of our faith . . . we have to go back to the New Testament." Assuring the Jewish people in the room he would never offend them "for anything," Roberts asserted that "the best things that Christians have to offer is to be Christians . . . when we Christians try to return to Judaism, we create more problems than we create help." According to Roberts Jr., Paul wrote the book of Galatians to get Christians to "stop worrying about all that law," and to show that "everything that happened in the OT was merely a foreshadow of what was to come." In the same vein, the New Testament was constantly touted as superior to the Old Testament.

The theology presented at this conference echoes that which resulted in history's most heinous acts of antisemitism. The deicide charge (the assertion that the Jewish people alone are responsible for the death of Christ and were eternally damned because of it), the Inquisition, the expulsions, the ghettos, the pogroms, the gas chambers—these atrocities resulted, either directly or indirectly, from a triumphalist Christianity. The Apostle Paul, in his letter to the Romans, warns Gentile believers about this very kind of arrogance. He writes, "do not brag that you are better than those branches [unbelieving Jewish people]" (11:18) after having been grafted into the olive tree themselves (11:17b). Prior to this warning, Paul assures the Gentiles of the Jewish people's continued role as God's chosen people, even with their rejection of Jesus the Messiah. He writes, "has God rejected His people? Absolutely not!" (11:1). Because the Gentiles have been grafted in with Jewish believers, they "share in the rich root of the cultivated olive tree" (11:17b). Thus, the church is made up of both Gentile and Jewish believers (Ephesians 2:11–22). The national, ethnic Israel, however, remains a unique and separate entity from the church.

As a result of being grafted into the olive tree, Gentile believers are included in the spiritual blessings of the Abrahamic covenant (Genesis 12:1–3) through the New Covenant (Jeremiah 31:31–40; Luke 22:20).

What are the spiritual blessings of the covenant? Salvation, forgiveness of sin, union with Christ, and eternal life, among others. Notice that the spiritual blessings do not include the land promise. The land promise is made to ethnic, national Israel, and Israel alone. The land is given to them by God (Genesis 12; 13; 17) and that promise still stands (Romans 9:4; 11:28).

Note well: Christian triumphalism is sinful. Christians must heed Paul's words and avoid arrogance regarding their standing as those who were grafted in. Christians should avoid prioritizing the New Testament over the Old—they are equally the Word of God (2 Timothy 3:16), and the Old Testament is the foundation of both the New Testament and of our faith. Christians should also avoid scoffing at Judaism (specifically, biblical Judaism), as Christianity's roots are buried deep within biblical Judaism. Our Lord and King is the Jewish Messiah promised by the Old Testament. His disciples were Jewish, and so too were the members of the early church. Christianity has no room for triumphalism.

Not only was the conference's theology antisemitic, the politics were too. The leaders of CATC hammered home the injustices of what they called the "Israeli occupation of Palestine." They are not alone in holding this political view. Many people who are on the left politically see Israel as an occupier and the Palestinians as an oppressed people. The truth is, the Israeli-Palestinian conflict is incredibly complex. Both sides—the Israelis and the Palestinians—have legitimate hurts, claims, and stories regarding the land of Israel. That being said, Christians must take a nuanced approach when it comes to truly understanding the conflict. A nuanced approach examines all aspects of a claim. Take the claim that Israel is an apartheid state, for example. Proponents of this view point to the concrete border wall, the checkpoints, and the discrimination against Palestinians as proof of Israeli apartheid. A closer look, however, would reveal something different. The wall separating the West Bank and Gaza from Israel proper was built after waves of terrorist attacks in the early 2000s killed many Israeli civilians. In order to prevent more loss of life, Israel built the wall. Since the wall's construction, terrorism has decreased by 90 percent.[8] It is important to note that only about 20 percent of the wall is made of concrete—the rest is fence. Checkpoints, too, were instituted for the same reason: to prevent terrorists from entering Israel proper, not as instruments of discrimination.

When it comes to Israeli treatment of Palestinians, a nuanced view is also required. Arab-Israelis comprise 21 percent of Israel's total population.[9] These Arabs are full citizens of Israel and enjoy the rights of full citizens. Furthermore, the majority of Palestinians live under Palestinian governance, either in the West Bank or Gaza. The West Bank, which is split into three areas—Area A, Area B, and Area C—is the home of some three million Palestinians. Most Palestinians live in Area A, which is governed by the Palestinian Authority. Some two million Palestinians live in Gaza, which is controlled by the Palestinian terror group Hamas.[10] If any party is responsible for the suffering of Palestinians, it is the Palestinian leadership. It is also true to say Arabs do face some measure of discrimination in Israel. There is certainly work to be done in this area. However, Israel is the freest country in the Middle East: its leaders are elected by the people, and its citizens enjoy religious and civil freedoms, a growing economy, and wonderful medical and educational systems. It is far from an apartheid state.

A nuanced approach also considers the way in which accusations like apartheid might affect Israel and the Jewish people as a whole. One practical outworking of this view of Israel is the BDS movement. The leaders of CATC openly praised the BDS movement[11] and encouraged

---

[8] Mitchell Bard, "West Bank, Gaza and Lebanon Security Barriers: Background and Overview," Jewish Virtual Library, accessed October 5, 2020, https://www.jewishvirtuallibrary.org/background-and-overview-of-israel-s-security-fence.

[9] "Vital Statistics: Latest Population Statistics for Israel," accessed October 5, 2020, https://www.jewishvirtuallibrary.org/latest-population-statistics-for-israel.

[10] Khaled Abu Toameh, "Palestinian Consensus: 4.7 Million in West Bank and Gaza," *Times of Israel*, accessed October 5, 2020, https://www.timesofisrael.com/palestinian-census-4-7-million-in-west-bank-and-gaza-strip/.

[11] https://bdsmovement.net/what-is-bds.

conference attendees to participate in it themselves. According to their website, BDS seeks to Boycott, Divest, and Sanction the state of Israel in order to end Israeli occupation of Palestine by encouraging consumer boycotts of companies that are complicit in the occupation of Palestine.[12] BDS also encourages colleges, churches, and cities to disengage from Israel "academically, culturally, economically and militarily."[13] The problem with BDS, aside from pushing an unfair narrative, is its results. When an Israeli company is boycotted and forced to close, both Israelis and Palestinians lose their jobs.[14] When universities pass BDS legislation, Jewish students become targets of cruel antisemitism.[15] A movement that causes such injustices should be avoided by Christians.

The antisemitic, anti-Israel positions propagated at Christ at the Checkpoint are only becoming more mainstream within the church as Christians who want to pursue justice fall into unjust thinking. As Christians we are called to seek justice—true justice. When it comes to the Jewish people and Israel, true justice acknowledges the rich Jewish roots of Christianity, and the history of Christian antisemitism. True justice rejects Christian triumphalism. True justice empathizes with the suffering of both Israeli Jews and Palestinians, without blaming only one party for the suffering. True justice allows theology to inform politics, not the opposite. Most importantly, true justice stems from a true and deep love for Jesus, our Jewish Messiah.

---

[12] "What is BDS," accessed October 5, 2020, https://bdsmovement.net/what-is-bds.

[13] Palestinian BDS National Committee, "Join the BDS Movement and Make an Impact," accessed October 5, 2020, https://bdsmovement.net/make-an-impact.

[14] David Horovitz, "Victory for BDS as SodaStream's Last Palestinian Workers Lose Their Jobs," *Times of Israel*, accessed October 5th, 2020, https://www.timesofisrael.com/victory-for-bds-as-sodastreams-last-palestinian-workers-lose-their-jobs/.

[15] Editors of *The Algemeiner*, "The 40 Worst Colleges for Jewish Students, 2017," accessed October 5, https://www.algemeiner.com/the-40-worst-colleges-for-jewish-students-2017/.

## ABOUT THE AUTHOR

Brittany Bertsche is a graduate student at the University of Haifa, where she is pursuing her master's degree in Holocaust studies. She graduated from Moody Bible Institute in 2019 with a bachelor's degree in Jewish studies. She has written articles about antisemitism, the Israeli-Palestinian conflict, and Christian Zionism. She coauthored an op-ed called "The Return of Christian Anti-Semitism," published in *The Detroit Jewish News*. She has led three trips to Israel for Christian college students in recent years. She is passionate about Jewish-Christian relations, advocacy against antisemitism, educating the church on the Jewish roots of Christianity, good books, and good coffee.

*Chapter Four*

# A BRIEF HISTORY OF ANTISEMITISM

### by
### David Meola, PhD

Many of this volume's contributing authors are giving more personal stories related to antisemitism. In this chapter, I intend to present a brief introduction on antisemistim and its historical origins.

The term "antisemitism" officially dates to the year 1879, when Wilhelm Marr—a notable Hamburg Liberal[16]—wrote the pamphlet *The Victory of Jewry over Germandom*. In this piece, Marr wrote the following:

> Jewry's control of society and politics, as well as its practical domination of religious and ecclesiastical thought, is still in the prime of its development. . . . Your generation will not pass before there will be absolutely no public office, even the highest one, which the Jews will not have usurped.

> German culture has proved itself ineffective and powerless against this foreign power. . . . We have among us a flexible,

---

[16] It should be noted that Liberals in Germany were not the same as British or American liberals and were generally far more conservative politically and socially.

tenacious, intelligent, foreign tribe that knows how to bring abstract reality into play in many different ways. Not individual Jews, but the Jewish spirit and Jewish consciousness have overpowered the world.[17]

Marr's diatribe against German citizens, in particular, of Jewish faith and world Jewry was not the first piece to ascribe such "power" or "insidiousness" to Jews. While the term antisemitism is only about 140 years old, the sentiment that Marr captures goes back through the ages. It is important to understand, however, that while there are continuities in anti-Jewish/antisemitic feelings throughout time, there are enough differences that warrant a careful consideration about how we label events and attitudes in the past.

In the Euro-American world, the roots of antisemitism come from polytheistic society's inability to accept that Jews worshiped a singular deity and their claim of "chosen-ness." Greeks in Alexandria forced Jews of the city to live in a Jewish quarter and they also fomented riots against Jews. In Ancient Rome, Jews fared slightly better and were generally protected by the emperor. Yet, even there, intolerance led to the imposition of Roman symbols in the Second Temple, a desecration that led to revolt, the destruction of the Second Temple in 70 CE, and forced dispersion. As historian Eric Gruen argues, however, Jews were already a diaspora before the conclusion of the first century. Anti-Jewish animus followed Jews to their new communities, but it did not drastically increase in the Roman Empire until Christianity became the official imperial religion. While several emperors were ambivalent about Jews' official status in the empire, there were others who enacted harsh legislation. During the Theodosian period (379–457 CE), for example, emperors stripped

---

[17] Wilhelm Marr, "The Victory of Jewry over Germandom," in *The Jew in the Modern World: A Documentary History*, 3rd ed., edited by Paul Mendes-Flohr and Jehuda Reinharz (Oxford: Oxford University Press, 2011), 306–7.

Jews of rights accorded to other citizens and reduced Jews to a marginal existence.

Church doctrine and the teachings of St. Augustine, who believed that Jews should live in penury for rejecting Christ, inspired much of the public animus against Jews during this period. Some scholars view Augustine's anti-Jewish views as more moderate than other Christian scholars of his time, since Augustine did not believe Jews should be killed.[18] Nonetheless, the idea of Jewish inferiority and perniciousness pervaded Christian thought for centuries. As changes occurred in the Christian world, anti-Jewish rhetoric helped inform violence against Jews, including expulsion and forced conversion.

After the Roman period, Jewish life in Europe was not easy, and their situation worsened as the world around them fragmented into decentralized empires and religious fiefdoms. During the Middle Ages, and especially during the vitriolic fervor of the Crusading era, Jews were often the target of horrific antisemitic violence and expulsions. In the German city of Worms (present-day Germany), among others, Crusaders rounded up Jews and locked them into their synagogue, which was then set ablaze. Toward the end of the crusading period, the Spanish monarchs launched an inquisition, in which Jews were exiled from Spain in 1492 in order to prevent Jewish converts (Marranos) from backsliding to Judaism.

Alongside this crusading fervor, anti-Jewish tropes—preached from on high—also led to mass suspicion of Jews. In 1144, Jews were first accused of a "blood libel" against William of Norwich. The blood libel myth accuses Jews of sacrificing Christian children and using their blood to make Passover matzoh, a virulent indictment with no historical accuracy or evidence. The most famous so-called blood libel in the late medieval period involved the three-year-old Simon of Trent. Not only did authorities blame and then murder twelve members of that Jewish community, but the child was beatified by the Church. Blood libel accusations

---

[18] John Efron, Matthias Lehmann, and Steven Weitzman, *The Jews: A History*, 3rd ed. (New York and London: Routledge, 2019), 125.

resurfaced during the nineteenth century, and variants of this canard are still in use by antisemites today.

Another pernicious belief that still resonates from medieval Europe is the association of Jews and disease. During the bubonic plague in the fourteenth century, Church officials and members of the public accused Jews of spreading the disease and poisoning the wells. In response to these accusations, authorities tortured Jews until they gave up the names of individuals "responsible" for such acts, while other Jewish communities were persecuted and banished. Such a trope was used time and again—Jews were blamed for the spread and transmission of syphilis at the end of the nineteenth century, the Nazis explicitly tied Jews to disease and poison (as seen in the children's story, *Der Giftpilz* [The Poisonous Mushroom]), and today there are people who believe Jews are responsible for the creation and transmission of, and profiting from, the novel coronavirus (COVID-19).

As these examples indicate, antisemites before 1500 often targeted Jews for their religious difference. Their ability to scapegoat Jews for unexplained phenomena proved a useful way to justify religious zealots' drive for purity. Even as the Reformation dramatically changed Europe, hatred against Jews remained. Martin Luther, progenitor of the Reformation, wrote "Concerning the Jews and their Lies" (1543) and not only reiterated many falsehoods about Jews, but also called for Jews to be expelled and/or killed, with their synagogues burned to the ground and churches erected on top of the remnants.[19] Later, religious scholars viewed Judaism as "fossilized," or saw Jews as "ahistorical" and living "out of time." In one of the most pernicious pieces of antisemitic scholarship, Johann Eisenmenger's *Entdecktes Judentum* (1700, *Jewry Revealed*) directly attacked the Talmud, and believed this text directed Jews "to cheat and injure Christians through usury; that Jews were either incapable of taking up noncommercial occupations or unwilling to; that belief in a Messiah who would lead Jews back to rule in Zion prevented them

---

[19] Efron et al., 235–236.

from feeling patriotic attachment to their countries of residence."[20] Such scholars believed that the only way Jews could achieve redemption and salvation was through conversion.

Toward the end of the eighteenth century, antisemitic thought evolved to reflect both Enlightenment values and those ideas that rejected the Enlightenment's rationalizing impulses. Historian Steven Beller has called such variants "irrationalist" and "rationalist." The irrational form rejects the Enlightenment's drive for knowledge and often dovetailed with Romanticism's search for "origins" and rejection of industrialization. Richard Wagner was emblematic of this type of thought. The famous composer regularly attacked Jewish inauthenticity and mimesis of European tastes. The rejection of industrialization and capitalism (or "Manchesterism" as it was also called) was also a rejection of Jews' role in the modern world. Antisemites were quick to tie Jews to the ill-effects of the modern, capitalist, and industrial world, building off of age-old associations of Jews with money (for instance, Shylock in Shakespeare's *Merchant of Venice*). Even more modern ideologies, such as socialism and communism, made this association, as seen in Marx's 1844 essay, *Zur Judenfrage* ("On the Jewish Question"). In this manner, irrationalist critique denied individualism and secularism as the basis of society, and instead promoted a collective and/or mythical nation.

While irrationalist antisemitism built off centuries of anti-Jewish hatred, rationalist antisemitism used new Enlightenment ideas about race to frame their arguments, including the idea that Jews had lesser and more superficial mental faculties, and that their bodies were effeminate and inferior to that of Aryans'.[21] This science of race merged easily with the rise of nationalism and the new era of imperialism. Nation-states became codetermined by land and a discernible, unique people,

---

[20] Brian E. Vick, *Defining Germany: The 1848 Frankfurt Parliamentarians and National Identity* (Cambridge, Massachusetts: Harvard University Press, 2002), 85.
[21] Steven Beller, *Antisemitism: A Very Short Introduction*, 2nd ed. (Oxford: Oxford University Press, 2015), 58.

so heterogenous states like Austria-Hungary struggled, while more homogenous states like Germany thrived. States with imperialist visions of glory, like the new German Empire (1871), used rationalist racial logic to order their worlds, yet it had a reciprocal influence: not only was race ordered in far-away colonies, it was also restructured at home. As nations embraced collective identities, Jews were often seen as pernicious elements that prevented groups from achieving success. In Vienna, citizens blamed Jews for the economic problems among the people; in France, Parisians and rural subjects blamed Jews for the loss of prestige and honor, and among aspiring nations, Jews were seen as oppressive agents of imperial powers. As a result of these associations, antisemitism thrived throughout Europe. At the turn of the twentieth century, Karl Lueger ran an explicitly antisemitic campaign to win the mayoralty of Vienna, French artillery captain Alfred Dreyfus was falsely convicted for treason (for selling military secrets to the Germans), and an antisemitic pogrom killed or injured over five hundred Jews in Kishinev and left two thousand Jews homeless. In addition to these dramatic events, renewed blood libel accusations became more common, which also put Jews' lives in danger.[22] We see that while the rationalist antisemitism grew rapidly, the irrationalist elements never went away.

Many Jews left Europe to find safer homes, yet even in these locations, Jew-hatred and antisemitism could be found. Even though one of the most notorious antisemitic incidents happened during the US Civil War—when General Grant expelled the Jews "as a class" from Kentucky—the twentieth century saw more violent displays. In 1915, Leo Frank was lynched in Atlanta, Henry Ford bought the *Dearborn Independent* and used it as an anti-Jewish propaganda machine, and antisemitism (along with xenophobia) underpinned the rise of the America First Party. There were many places in the United States—especially hotels—which would not accommodate Jews. While the level of antisemitism in

---

[22] See, for instance, Helmut Walser Smith, *The Butcher's Tale: Murder and Anti-Semitism in a German Town* (New York: W.W. Norton, 2002).

the United States never reached the fervor that it did in Europe, the pervasiveness of antisemitism structured the lack of an American response during the Nazi era.

After World War I, antisemitism around the world reached new heights, though its most virulent strain would rise in Germany. During World War I, Jews were framed as unpatriotic and as shirking military duty. As Germany's war efforts failed, the military leadership blamed Jews for suing for peace and accepting Germany's culpability for war— the "stab in the back" legend *(Dolchstosslegende)*. In 1920, a new party structured its policies around antisemitism—the National Socialist German Workers Party, otherwise known as the Nazi Party. Instead of creating a new form of antisemitism, the Nazis fused all of the available antisemitic strands into their own ideological platform. Fused with the disaster of the First World War, the multiple economic hardships affecting Germany during the 1920s, and the dramatic cultural shift after the war, this new, virulent antisemitism provided a foundation for the Nazis to blame all of society's ills on Jews and to position themselves as "saviors" of the Aryan race. Once the Nazis were democratically elected in 1933, German Jews' fate was sealed. In the end, approximately six million Jews were murdered by the Nazis for the sole crime of having been born a Jew, and if not for the Allied Victory, all Jews around the world would have been in peril.

As a coda to this brief look at historical antisemitism, I want to leave you with a few thoughts.

- First, the Nazis were not monsters; they were human like you and me. The Holocaust, like other genocides past and present, was conceived and implemented by humans. Antisemitism was the basis for the Nazis, crimes, but it also was the foundation for German society's tacit acceptance of Jews' exclusion, excising, and murder. We should remember that such hatred is not specific to Jews, and that all racism is the basis for such heinous actions.

- Second, antisemitism is not consigned to the past. One could alternatively say that the era of 1945 to 2010 and its relative tranquility was an anomaly and not the norm. Antisemitic incidents are on the rise dramatically over the past five years, with a spike since 2016. This culminated in the attacks on the Tree of Life Synagogue in Pittsburgh; the shooting at a Poway, California, synagogue; and the 2017 Unite the Right rally in Charlottesville. The shooting in Pittsburgh was the deadliest antisemitic attack in US history. [23]

- Finally, I want to reiterate that latent antisemitism is just as insidious as active antisemitism, though its immediate manifestations are not as apparent. Microaggressions, over time, build up and structure how people react. Think about how many people across the world believed canards about Jews as a group and how that structured their (non-) actions during the Nazi period—whether that meant not admitting Jews as immigrants, or even refusing to associate as friends.

## ABOUT THE AUTHOR

Dr. David A. Meola is the Bert and Fanny Meisler Assistant Professor of History and Jewish Studies at the University of South Alabama. He received his doctorate in history and master of European studies from the University of British Columbia in Vancouver, Canada, and holds a bachelor of science in business administration from the University of North Carolina in Chapel Hill. His research focuses on German-Jewish life and religious reform, antisemitism, and the burgeoning German liberal and democratic movement during the 1840s. Dr. Meola has published articles and chapters in *Antisemitism Studies* and the *Leo Baeck Institute Yearbook*, and he has a manuscript under review at Indiana University Press. In addition to his research, Dr. Meola loves college sports (go Heels!), drinking espresso, cooking and grilling, traveling, and spending time with his wife and four children.

---

[23] For more on antisemitism statistics, go to www.adl.org.

*Chapter Five*

# A RENDEZVOUS WITH DESTINY IN BUS #18

### by
### Yisroel Stefansky

fter reading the title of this chapter, you might be asking how a bus could become the decisive moment in a person's life, but events out of our control can often shape and define destiny. It seems surreal now as a forty-year-old to think about the awful day in my childhood when a bus would radically alter my life's direction. I know for certain if I had never boarded bus #18, my future would have been different. I wish the event I am talking about would have never happened, but this I cannot change. I also cannot change the ever-present and gnawing memory of the bomb blast that shattered a beautiful spring morning in March 1996. I want to tell you how my world was broken on that spring day in bus #18, but first I want to give you a glimpse of my world that was.

My father, Abraham Stefansky, is a Holocaust survivor. At the close of WWII, he immigrated to the United States, married, and started a new life in New York City. Not long after the Six-Day War in 1967, my mother and father, along with many other Jews, made Aliyah to Israel. My parents followed in the Orthodox Jewish tradition of having a large family and bore eight sons. I was the sixth son to be born, and I was born in Jerusalem.

My father was instrumental in building an ultra-Orthodox college called Neve Yerushalayim in the Har Nof neighborhood of Jerusalem. Today, it is the oldest and largest college for Jewish women in the world, with over one thousand students and thirty-five thousand alumni. The women come from Jewish communities around the world to study the Torah, history, philosophy, Jewish law, and the art of kosher cooking. Quite often, they are matched to a Jewish young man in one of the many yeshiva schools for men around Jerusalem. At eighty-seven years old, my father continues to work in the administration of the college. I often drive him there in his Subaru Forester.

I was raised in the ultra-Orthodox Unsdorf neighborhood in Jeru-salem, where I still live today. My parents live there, as well. These have been my surroundings since birth, and I enjoyed a sheltered and pro-tected childhood filled with kosher food, peaceful Sabbaths, Yiddish humor, classical music, and books—always books. My fondest memories as a young boy include seeing my mother light the Sabbath candles and then feel the tender hands of my father upon my head blessing me with the blessing of Ephraim and Manasseh, the smell of the warm Challah bread just under the white napkin surrounded by my mother's finest dishes and the setting sun reflecting the golden Jerusalem stone through our dining room window. It was as if the busy world was hushed for that moment. And for the Stefansky family, the cares of life did vanish with the vanishing of the sun over the mountains of Jerusalem every Sabbath. To picture the environment in my neighborhood, just think of *Fiddler on the Roof* in an urban setting. I am a Sabra (native-born Israeli). My grandparents, Bruno and Lynn Stefansky, are buried in the Mount of Olives Cemetery near the Eastern Gate of the Old City. They wanted to be close to where the Messiah will enter Jerusalem at the resurrection.

Tragically, the peaceful hamlet my parents created for me was shat-tered like a broken glass under the heel of a groom at a Jewish wedding. The breach in the barricade surrounding our family and protecting us from the outside world's hatred of our people and our way of life came suddenly, without warning. We always assumed Jerusalem would be a safe haven for our family. We earnestly believed the tentacles of anti-semitism that clawed toward my father during the Holocaust could never reach into the small ultra-Orthodox community of Unsdorf within the gates of Jerusalem. We were wrong.

On a peaceful Sunday morning, March 3, 1996, at 6:20 a.m., at the age of fifteen, I was on my way to school. That's when the safety net around my world was ripped open. I was standing at the intersection of Jaffa Road and Kings of Israel Road. There was a red light in the pedestrian cross-walk, and as I waited, bus #18 approached the intersection and slowed to a stop because the traffic light in front of it turned red. I secured my school backpack over my shoulder, preparing to cross Jaffa Road as soon as I had the right of way. What I didn't know was at that moment, a suicide bomber viciously wanting to shed innocent Jewish blood was aboard bus #18 just a few meters away from where I stood. As soon as I took my first step into the crosswalk, the terrorist aboard the bus detonated the explosives wrapped tightly around his body. In Israel, you must understand that Sunday is a busy workday, so at that time of the morning, the buses are packed with students, soldiers, children on their way to school, office workers, mothers, fathers, and the elderly.

When the bomb went off, I felt the sidewalk beneath me quake, and my ears began to echo with ringing from the blast. As I saw the flames and heard the screams, my first thought was that it must be a scene in a movie. Remember, I was a fifteen-year-old sheltered Jewish kid. Rarely had I ventured out of my protected hamlet. I could never imagine that people could or would blow other people up in buses—especially in my little neighborhood of Unsdorf. I knew nothing of hate, or war, or bloodshed. I did my schoolwork, studied Torah, excelled in different languages, wore the kippah and tallit, read Jewish history and philosophy, and honored my father and mother.

In a split second, I realized this was not a scene from an action movie, and at that moment, I did something I still do not understand to this day. Hearing a powerful explosion like that and seeing the wounded stagger from a burning bus, a person's first inclination would be to run away from the flames. This I didn't do. Instead, I dropped my school bag and ran toward the bus. It was as if I had an epiphany or revelation that I was to help save the wounded. I felt something pushing me in the direction of the bus. As I ran, I remember seeing an object flying toward me. Before I reached the bus, I realized the object was a human leg because it fell on the street directly in my path.

Though it was not a movie, it certainly felt like one. Time slowed, and I entered the world of the surreal. I climbed into the bus, and there were body parts strewn about everywhere, and blood was dripping from the ceiling and seats. People were screaming. Children were crying. Wounded elderly moaned and writhed in shock and agony. The air was filled with smoke and the smell of smoldering flesh. It was difficult to breathe. I heard the cries of mothers searching for their children. I saw school books and school bags covered in blood strewn about. I did all I could do in those moments to help the wounded off of the bus.

In Israel, during these years of relentless suicide bombings, we classified wounded as missing a limb or a body part. So, the losses were horrific. When the first and second intifadas finally ceased, there were 1,300 Jewish men, women, and children murdered and 8,000 wounded. Most of the causalities came from suicide bombings, but the terrorists also used planted bombs. Many Jews were stabbed, shot, or stoned to death, and some were lynched.

When the first responders came, I stepped off bus #18, gathered my books, and did the only thing I knew to do: I finished my walk to school. As I walked, I looked down at my clothes and hands; I was covered in blood. I remember thinking the rest of that day as I sat in class how ill-equipped I felt on that bus. If I knew how to tie a tourniquet or perform CPR (in a suicide bomb attack, some people perish not because of wounds from the explosion but because their hearts stop from the pressure of the blast), maybe I could have saved more lives. Somehow I knew my life would never be the same. The world as I knew it ended on that March morning in 1996. My childhood innocence had been stripped from me. The explosion on bus #18 became the defining moment of my life from the second that suicide bomber pressed the trigger until today.

At the age of fifteen, somehow, I knew more bombings were sure to come, so instead of playing basketball and being involved in the normal activities of kids my age, I began to study how to save lives. Each day after school and into the evening hours, I attended training sessions hosted by Magen David Adom, Israel's national emergency medical, disaster, ambulance, and blood bank service. The name means "Red Shield of David." At the age of sixteen, I completed my EMT (Emergency Medical Technician) training, and by the time the second wave of the Intifada began in 2000, I was better prepared.

I think when the world hears of another terror attack in Israel, they disregard it mainly because there is nothing personal about it. It's just another statistic in the daily news cycle like a brush fire or flood in some far off corner of the world. By its nature, the news does not focus on what is lost in a suicide attack but rather on how it was lost: "A suicide bomber carrying ten kilos of explosives blew himself up, killing ten Israelis and wounding fourteen." So, we know what method the terrorist used to kill, how many he killed, and how many he wounded. We've learned to divorce ourselves from the harrowing pain of what is lost in the mass murder of Jews and categorize the events into numbers, and kilograms, and collateral damage reports. We do the same with the Holocaust. Six million dead. End of story. We forget the six million were actually human souls who lived and loved—musicians, poets, historians, rabbis, mothers, fathers, children (many infants), bubbies and zadies (grandmothers and grandfathers). In their extermination, we lost future generations—forever! So I think we should focus on what is lost when a life is taken rather than just on how it was lost.

For me, at the moment bus #18 exploded, I lost my childhood innocence. Some have asked me if I lost my faith, and I say no. I understand why evil has always been thirsty for Jewish blood. We Jews brought G-d's moral law into the world, and for this, the world has never forgiven us.

It is not just that evil people hate Jews—they ultimately hate the G-d of the Jews. As His Chosen People, burdened with the responsibility of being His light of revelation to the nations—we, in turn, are despised by the nations, in turn. I heard someone once say, because the Jewish people wrote down and preserved G-d's commandments, they are like the world's alarm clock that awakens it to its accountability to the righteous standards of G-d, and not everyone appreciates being jarred awake by an alarm clock. This is why Jews have been detested and scorned for ages. By rejecting us, the antisemite believes he can somehow repudiate and nullify the righteous commandments of G-d. The conflict the world has with Israel is not about land. It's about Jews and the G-d of the Jews. Israel's enemies not only call for the extermination of the Jewish people in Israel but promote a global ethnic cleansing of all Jews everywhere. They believe by erasing us, they erase the one true G-d.

Since that fateful day in March of 1996, I have responded to over fifty terror attacks in Israel. I remember the details of each one. I remember because innocent human lives were lost. I want to share with you what I saw, heard, and felt in a number of these attacks. I want there to be a record of what actually happened behind the scenes so that the next time Jewish blood is spilled, you will share in our suffering, pain, and grief for the lost and wounded.

On Saturday night, December 1, 2001, I responded to a triple terror attack in downtown Jerusalem that killed eleven people. I remember entering the scene of the attack, the Café Riomn, and seeing friends of mine who were wounded having no concern for themselves and trying to help others. This was one of the most courageous things I have ever witnessed.

After our first responders tended to the dying and injured and the last ambulance departed for the hospital, I traded my EMT vest for another vest—the vest of a ZAKA volunteer. I joined this organization when the second Intifada began because I believed in their holy work. ZAKA is a Hebrew acronym that describes the mission of identifying victims of terror. You see, according to Halacha, the collection of Jewish religious laws, a deceased body of a Jewish person must be buried in as a complete state as possible. This requires the body to retain its blood and as many parts of its anatomy as possible at the time of burial. This comes from Genesis 3:19: "From dust you came and to dust you shall return." This is a terrible issue to even speak about, but let me just say that the scene of a suicide attack is covered with body parts, blood, and human entrails. After the wounded were sped away to the hospital, ZAKA volunteers—many of them first responders as well—descended on the scene to do the holy and religious work of putting bodies back together, according to Halacha. The scene became a forensic lab of sorts as we measured the distance between torsos and heads, limbs, and fingers. We matched body parts by skin tones and clothes. We each had scrapers in our utility bags to scrape blood from the floors of restaurants, buses, coffee shops, and streets so that we could return the blood to the nearest body. The atmosphere was sober, quiet, and respectful. Instead of a place of violence, we turned it into a place of honoring the souls of the victims. Through our quiet work, we came to realize the depth of what was lost in these attacks. Today there are over 3,500 ZAKA volunteers in Israel that continue this reverent service after terror attacks. That Israel, a country the size of New Jersey, requires this many volunteers to bury those murdered by Islamic terror attacks, should awaken the world to the constant burden of terror Israelis bear.

On Saturday night, March 9, 2002, there was a suicide bomber attack in Jerusalem at the Café Moment restaurant, killing eleven. It was tough to see young adults sitting around tables with no visible injuries yet dead because their hearts had stopped from the impact of the bomb. On the same night, another terror attack took place in the city of Netanya, a beach town on the central coast of Israel. Here, a nine-month-old little girl perished along with a twenty-seven-year-old young man who was a member of our first responders and one of my classmates. I took this very hard.

One Saturday night, in March of 2002, there was a terror attack not far from my neighborhood. When I arrived at the scene, I came upon a stroller, but there was no baby in it because the blast had blown the baby out of the stroller. I remember frantically searching for the baby as if it were my own. I found the baby in the middle of the street. The baby was a little girl but had passed away. The face of this precious little girl remains locked in my memory bank, and I never want to forget her. Today she would be about eighteen years of age. Her life was taken away because she was Jewish.

On Tuesday evening, September 9, 2003, a father took his daughter out for coffee in the evening at the Café Hillel restaurant in Jerusalem. The next morning, the daughter was to be married. The father was a doctor and the head of the emergency room at Shaare Zedek hospital in Jerusalem. That night, seven souls were lost in the Café Hillel, including the father and his daughter because of a senseless suicide bomb. The attack was perpetrated by Hamas member Ramez Abu Salim.

In 2004, eight years after the explosion of bus #18, I founded a program called Advanced Security Training Institute (ASTI) that combines the real-world experiences of Israeli counterterrorism and disaster response with training from experts in the field. The program was developed to allow agencies abroad the chance to study and understand the lessons learned from decades of long exposure to attacks and disasters in Israel.

Our staff is made up of American and Israeli counterterrorism experts, medical professionals, and disaster management professionals. The experience of the ASTI training staff is unparalleled, as there is no place on earth like Israel, where disasters have been so heavily experienced. This also means that there is no other place on the planet where counterterrorism and disaster management have become as sophisticated.

As our world becomes more connected, and in some cases further divided, emergency managers, police, and fire and medical personnel are going to increasingly face the types of disasters and attacks that have affected Israel for decades. We want to help police, firemen, medical professionals, and emergency management personnel discover new preparedness and operational strategy to respond and train their teams to be more effective. Our mission is to simply save lives in every community across America.

First responders in the United States have an opportunity to learn from the challenging experiences that Israelis have already encountered. The ASTI training program seeks to share that information and insight broadly so that personnel in the United States are better prepared to help their citizens in times of need. Because together, we can save lives. We are training today for a safer tomorrow.

It says in the Talmud, "He who saves one life saves the world entire." I have lived by this principle every day since my experience as a young fifteen-year-old Jewish boy running toward bus #18. Fighting to save Jewish lives in the face of growing antisemitism has become my *tikun olam* in Hebrew—my way to try and make the world a better place.

Now that you know my story, I hope you will consider the grief and pain the Jews continue to experience because of the murderous violence and rage inspired by antisemitism. I am confident you will breathe a prayer for those suffering loss when you hear of another violent terror attack against Jews—be it in Israel or in other parts of the world. If anyone should be the messengers of the loss suffered by terror, it should be the dead who suffered the greatest loss. But these messengers cannot speak because their voices have been silenced. So what is our role? By remembering and retelling their stories, we become, in the words of Elie Wiesel, the messengers' messengers.

## ABOUT THE AUTHOR

Yisroel Stefansky is the president and founder of The Advanced Security Training Institute (ASTI). Yisroel is a recognized expert in practical disaster response and is an international lecturer in the field of counter-terrorism. He has appeared on CNN, KTVT, Fox News, Israel National News, Radio Israel, and CFRB Toronto. As a young man, Stefansky found himself at the site of a violent terror attack in Jerusalem. Rather than run from the scene, he took action and became part of the rescue effort. This experience led him to work with ZAKA, an organization that carries out the important and difficult task of recovering body parts for burial after a terror attack. Today, Stefansky's organization, ASTI, provides critical training for US members of Congress and US first responders in the areas of school safety, counterterrorism, and cybersecurity in an Israel-based immersion training course.

*Chapter Six*

# THE PALESTINIAN APPROPRIATION
# OF BLACK PAIN[24]

**by**

**Joshua Washington**

M y sisters and I grew up in a Hebrew Roots Christian household, which simply means that we grew up in a Christian household that embraced the Hebrew roots of our faith. My father and mother always taught us to appreciate the fact that without the Jewish faith, there would be no Christian faith. So, for me, there was always a spiritual connection to my Jewish friends, although many found us to be "weird," but we were used to that, as many of our Christian friends shared the same sentiment. The fact that we observe Shabbat and the feasts on the Hebrew calendar and did not celebrate Christmas or Easter, two of Christianity's biggest holidays, raised eyebrows. Over the years, however, it has also created a lot of deep and meaningful relationships between us and our Jewish brothers and sisters. It was not until my late teens and early twenties that I had more exposure to modern-day Israel,

---

[24] Portions of this chapter first appeared in the June 8, 2020 edition of *The Times of Israel*, https://blogs.timesofisrael.com/the-palestinian-appropriation-of-black-pain/

the intensity surrounding it, and later, the civil rights activists who were strong and loud Zionists.

In the early 1980s, Clayborne Carson, African-American professor of history at Stanford University and director of the Martin Luther King Jr. Research and Education Institute, published a paper called "Blacks and Jews in the Civil Rights Movement: The Case of SNCC."[25] In this paper, Carson gives much-needed clarity on Black-Jewish relations in the US, and what caused tensions to rise. Arguably, the most visible issue that caused conflict according to Carson was the Student Nonviolent Coordinating Committee's (SNCC) publication of "The Palestine Problem," a paper that sent a very loud and clear message to their Jewish supporters and Jews everywhere that so long as Jews supported a Jewish state, they were SNCC's enemies.

Caron's paper addresses this progression and gives crucial context to what otherwise seems like an abrupt shift in attitude. One thing Carson notes is the SNCC's biased investigation on the 1967 war. He writes:

> SNCC's Central Committee meeting in the midst of Israel's six-day victory over Arab forces in June 1967, requested that SNCC's search and communications staff investigate the background of the conflict. Ethel Minor, editor of SNCC's newsletter, volunteered for this task. She recalled that the committee wanted an "objective critique of the facts." Minor was not impartial on the issue, however, for she had been close friends with Palestinian students during her college years and was acquainted with the urban black nationalist tradition through her involvement with the Nation of Islam. Minor never wrote a position paper, nor did SNCC ever conduct an extended discussion of the Middle Eastern dispute.

---

[25] https://kinginstitute.stanford.edu/sites/mlk/files/blacks_jews_civil_rights.pdf

Carson says further:

> In the SNCC Newsletter, she listed thirty-two "documented facts" regarding "the Palestine Problem," including assertions that the Arab Israeli war was an effort to regain Palestinian land and that during the 1948 war, "Zionists conquered the Arab homes and land through terror, force, and massacres."

The newsletter[26] was full of falsehoods, many of which have long been categorically refuted. At the very least, a real investigation would mention the fact that Arab leaders were largely responsible for Palestinians leaving their homes, as they rejected compromise and launched a war to destroy the Jewish State.[27]

It would at least mention that Mizrahi Jews only arrived in Eretz, Israel, because they were expelled from the Middle Eastern and North African countries[28] they had been living in for generations. It would at least mention that there was always a Jewish presence in the Levant, and the small Jewish population in British Mandate Palestine at the time suffered many massacres at the hands of the Arabs simply for existing and being Jewish.

It is very clear that Minor's newsletter (complete with antisemitic drawings) was biased at best, and intentionally libelous and delegitimizing at worst. One might ask, besides the bias of having some Palestinian friends, why someone with as much gravitas as Ethel Minor would go through such great lengths to provoke and defame Israel and the Jewish people. The answer to that question has many layers.

SNCC, along with the rest of the Black community, were coming face-to-face with their radical progeny, and the tension from that was

---

[26] The Palestine Problem: Test Your Knowledge, https://www.crmvet.org/docs/sv/6707_sncc_news-r.pdf

[27] "Ethnic Cleansing" and pro-Arab Propaganda, https://www.haaretz.com/opinion/.premium-ethnic-cleansing-and-pro-arab-propaganda-1.5452143

[28] Rachel's Story, https://www.youtube.com/watch?v=sP4ON6xL39Q&t=7s

increasing more and more. Even radical Black Panther Stokely Carmichael in 1967 began distancing himself from SNCC, until 1968 when he left the group altogether. Many staff members at SNCC advocated for SNCC to break ties with their white and Jewish donors and change the vision of SNCC. The staff voted to declare that SNCC would henceforth be a "Human Rights Organization" that would "encourage and support the liberation struggles against colonization, racism, and economic exploitation around the world." Because of this change, SNCC felt that should apply to the Palestinians.

On March 25, 1968, just ten days before Martin Luther King was murdered, he participated in the annual convention of the Rabbinical Assembly. When Rabbi Everett Gendler asked King about the Black community's growing animus toward Jews and Israel, Dr. King said this:

> On the Middle East crisis, we have had various responses. The response of some of the so-called young militants again does not represent the position of the vast majority of Negroes. *There are some who are color-consumed and they see a kind of mystique in being colored, and anything non-colored is condemned. We do not follow that course in the Southern Christian Leadership Conference, and certainly most of the organizations in the civil rights movement do not follow that course.* [Emphasis added.]

King then goes on to proclaim his more famous quote in the Zionist world:

> I think it is necessary to say that what is basic and what is needed in the Middle East is peace. Peace for Israel is one thing. Peace for the Arab side of that world is another thing. Peace for Israel means security, and we must stand with all of our might to protect its right to exist, its territorial integrity. I see Israel, and never mind saying it, as one of the great outposts of democracy in the world, and a marvelous example of what can be done, how

desert land almost can be transformed into an oasis of brother-hood and democracy. Peace for Israel means security and that security must be a reality.

Then Dr. King pivots and addresses peace for the Palestinians (Palestinian was still a relatively new term at this point, so many referred to them generally as "Arabs"):

> On the other hand, we must see what peace for the Arabs means in a real sense of security on another level. Peace for the Arabs means the kind of economic security that they so desperately need. These nations, as you know, are part of that third world of hunger, of disease, of illiteracy. I think that as long as these conditions exist there will be tensions, there will be the endless quest to find scapegoats. *So there is a need for a Marshall Plan for the Middle East*, where we lift those who are at the bottom of the economic ladder and bring them into the mainstream of economic security. [Emphasis added.]

When quoting anyone, the context is just as important as the quote itself. Dr. King said the aforementioned quotes after the 1967 war between Israel and three neighboring Arab states. His quotes were made after SNCC published the baseless, biased, and belligerent newsletter. Dr. King's response was pro-Israel, pro-Arab, and pro-justice. It would seem that for an organization like SNCC to take such an anti-Israel stance would suggest they are the "color consumed" to whom King was referring—so caught up in the struggle against racism in the United States, they viewed everything through the American racist lens whether it truly applied or not. Yes, these Black militants ignored the atrocities carried out by the Palestinian Liberation Organization against their own people, and embraced Jew-hating, human-rights-abusing Yasser Arafat in the name of "justice." Dr. King said what he said in response to all of this.

In 1948, after World War II, the United States provided Western Europe with over $15 billion in aid. That is what is called the Marshall Plan. This is what King was referring to when he said there is a need for a Marshall Plan for the Middle East. Since 1949, the Palestinian Authority has received enough aid for some thirty Marshall Plans.[29] Even in the late 1960s, the PA had already received more than enough aid to climb up the economic ladder. One would think that a human rights organization like SNCC would inquire about why little has changed for the Palestinians and where the money is going; especially if said organization has taken upon itself to wade into the Israeli-Palestinian issue.

From then to Andrew Young's controversial resignation,[30] to Reverend Jesse Jackson's comradery with Yasser Arafat,[31] to Bayard Rustin's warning[32] to Black leaders about the dangers of not condemning PLO terrorism, the Black community became more and more split over the issue of Israel and the Jewish people.

Among the Black civil rights leaders, those who are anti-Israel tend to see a similarity between their struggle and the Palestinian struggle. Beside the fact that the notion is absolutely false,[33] it is intentional. Arab leaders have sought to hijack Black narratives to legitimize their cause since the '60s. That is why Mahmoud Abbas refers to Israel as "racist"

---

[29] United Nations Relief and Works Agency for Palestine Refugees in the Near East, https://www.unrwa.org/how-you-can-help/government-partners/funding-trends/donor-charts

[30] A Secret Meeting And a Very Public Exit at the U.N., https://www.nytimes.com/1979/08/19/archives/a-secret-meeting-and-a-very-public-exit-at-the-un.html

[31] Jesse Jackson, Advocating Talks With P.L.O., Meets Critics in Israel, https://www.nytimes.com/1979/09/25/archives/jesse-jackson-advocating-talks-with-plo-meets-critics-in-israel.html

[32] To Blacks: Condemn P.L.O. Terrorism, https://www.nytimes.com/1979/08/30/archives/to-blacks-condemn-plo-terrorism.html

[33] "7 Reasons Why the Palestinian Crisis and the Black Struggle for Freedom Are Absolutely Nothing Alike," https://blogs.timesofisrael.com/7-reasons-why-the-black-struggle-for-freedom-and-the-palestinian-crisis-are-absolutely-nothing-alike-by-a-black-man-whos-sick-and-tired-of-the-comparisons/

and compares it to Jim Crow laws America used to have. Such a propaganda campaign is only effective among the "color consumed." If one is color consumed, all Israel's enemies have to do is get them to see Israel as a country of white Europeans. Virtually nothing else has to be done; the color consumed will fill in the blanks with that very bias. It is why Mahmoud Abbas, president of the Palestinian Authority, calls Israel an "apartheid state," though nothing in Israel resembles apartheid. To the Black South African with unresolved hurt and bitterness from apartheid, not much else needs to be said.

The Palestinian appropriation of Black pain has gone on for decades, but there is sufficient reason to believe the organization Black Lives Matter in particular was not appropriated, but had antisemitism in its founding, as the founders themselves are self-proclaimed Marxists[34] who view Israel through the lens of color-consumed westerners, drawing parallels between Black Americans and Palestinians where there are none. In fact, our two plights could not be any different.

One of the biggest differences between Black Americans and Palestinians is terrorism. The Palestinian Authority encourages and incentivizes Palestinians to kill Jews.[35] Palestinians who successfully kill Jews are awarded with a monthly stipend from the PA. Palestinians who commit suicide while killing Jews have a monthly stipend sent to their families. Palestinian children[36] are trained to kill Jews by any means, including suicide bombing, and they are taught this through terrorist training camps[37]

---

[34] Martyn Iles, "'We Are Trained Marxists'—Patrisse Cullors, Co-Founder," YouTube, https://www.youtube.com/watch?v=HgEUbSzOTZ8.

[35] Palestinian Authority Paying Salaries to Terrorists with U.S. Money, https://www.gatestoneinstitute.org/2302/palestinian-authority-terrorist-salaries

[36] Kids on Hamas TV: "We want to die as Martyrs," https://www.youtube.com/watch?v=mue96rYTY7M

[37] Gaza Children Play War in Hamas Summer Camp, https://www.youtube.com/watch?v=9Pw8SO0GOJU

and Hamas TV shows.[38] Streets are named after Palestinians who commit suicide bombings if they kill enough Jews. The Black community has never resorted to any of these things. What the Palestinian Authority is engaged in is not a struggle against oppression; it is pure and simple Jew-hatred, and Palestinian leaders will do anything they can to legitimize it, including exploit Black pain to do so.

The more we at the Institute for Black Solidarity with Israel (IBSI) can uncover the truth concerning our common connection to the Jewish people, the easier it becomes to communicate to the misinformed. There is a pathway to peace for both the Israelis and Palestinians, and the Black community can play a key role in the effort toward peace. However, we in the Black community cannot even begin to have a discussion about a pathway to peace in Israel and Palestine until we come to the realization that our pain has been exploited in order to promote a false narrative. This is why I am honored to be included in this book with so many incredible authors. Together, we can let the truth ring out.

## ABOUT THE AUTHOR

Joshua David Washington is the director of the Institute for Black Solidarity with Israel (IBSI). He is a graduate of Christians United for Israel's 2016 Diversity Outreach Mentoring Endeavor (DOME), where he received training in Israel advocacy for diverse audiences. Joshua is a composition graduate of the University of Pacific's Conservatory of Music. Joshua served as IBSI's director of special events and planned music performances featuring The Hebrew Project Artists (THP) across the country. Joshua writes extensively about Zionism and civil rights, seeking to strengthen the Black and Jewish relationship in the United States. Joshua's articles appear regularly in *The Times of Israel*. Portions of this chapter first appeared in *The Times of Israel* on June 8, 2020.

---

[38] Kids shown video of their mother's suicide bombing death on Hamas TV, https://www.youtube.com/watch?v=XELcNMhkKCo

*Chapter Seven*

# GOD IS WATCHING: WHY AMERICA'S HISTORIC EMBRACE OF ANTISEMITISM MUST END

**by**

**Stuart Roth**

A s an attorney, one of the practice areas that I focus on is fighting antisemitism throughout the world. Over the last several years, this effort has focused largely on rebuffing the Boycott, Divestment, and Sanctions (BDS) movement, a campaign full of lies and deceit that is designed to delegitimize the State of Israel. The BDS movement here in the United States has been largely focused on fomenting antisemitism on our college campuses and introducing a new generation to the scourge of antisemitism and hatred of Jews. Many college students find themselves unequipped and without sufficient knowledge to address and combat antisemitism at school. They are bombarded by a segment of the student population whose core values are antisemitic, many of whom feel that Hitler didn't finish the "job."

While BDS leaders often try to describe themselves as "merely anti-Zionist," many of the central tenets of the BDS movement, as well as the statements of its leaders, are overtly antisemitic by any definition. But from a legal perspective, especially on campus, the definition that matters for so many reasons is the International Holocaust Remembrance Alliance (IHRA) definition. Among those reasons is what the IHRA organization represents.

IHRA is the only intergovernmental organization mandated to focus solely on Holocaust-related issues, and IHRA's member countries have pledged to commemorate the victims of the Holocaust, honoring their legacy and their memory.

Unfortunately, a lot of people today, especially young people, do not fully understand why this commitment is so incredibly important. People think that the Holocaust is just another part of ancient history, or that it doesn't matter because they themselves are not Jewish and therefore not immediately impacted. How painfully wrong they are.

The goal of Hitler's Holocaust was to eliminate Jews from every corner of the earth—to eradicate Jews wherever they could be found. However, this is not just a story about Jewish people. It is a horrifying warning about the effect that hatred and prejudice can have, and also about what happens when average people do not stand up and say, "Enough."

The Holocaust is one of the most, if not the most, extensively documented instances of atrocity, hatred, dehumanization, and apathy in world history. The world literally stood by and watched as Jews were hunted down throughout the world—their homes, property, and businesses stolen as they were rounded up like cattle and sent to concentration camps and gas chambers. No one was spared—women, children, elderly, and sick were raped, tortured, and brutalized before being sent to their death. The destruction of most of Europe's Jewish population occurred over more than twelve years as the world literally sat by and watched like spectators. It is well known that it was not only Hitler's soldiers that carried out the murder of over six million Jews, but that he had willing accomplices strategically placed all throughout the world, including the United States, that made it possible to round up and murder every Jew they could find on every continent the Nazis were able to infiltrate. It was a coordinated effort of evil not seen in modern times, orchestrated by many governments and ordinary citizens. This was a chapter of hatred that cannot be forgotten and swept under the rug. In this lesson lies the horror of a complacency of society when it fails to address racism and prejudice. America is no exception.

Antisemitism is nothing new to those here in the United States that are aware of its history. We can all read about recent attacks on Jewish synagogues and conspiracy theories of how Jews start pandemics or run Wall Street, Hollywood, or the media, but students today are rarely taught how Jews have had a long history of suffering the effect of racial, cultural, and religious hatred here in America.

Between 1880 and 1920, over three million Jews emigrated to the United States to escape persecution in Eastern Europe. They were not welcome here with open arms. In America, they found that many businesses and restaurants would not serve Jews, rent to Jews, or allow Jews to occupy certain professions. Jews were not permitted to join country clubs and civic organizations. Jews were excluded from living in certain communities or being treated at local hospitals or by certain physicians. Universities and colleges had strict quotas. My mother, who recently passed away at age ninety-one, received a letter from a college in the late 1940s rejecting her application on the grounds that they had already accepted their quota of Jews. Many colleges and universities had strict policies against hiring Jewish instructors and professors. Yes, that was here in the United States, and it was all considered legal.

The 1920s saw the rise of the Ku Klux Klan, which made Jews one of their targets. Henry Ford, founder of Ford Motor Company, was a virulent antisemite. He used his personal newspaper, *The Dearborn Independent*, as propaganda to poison minds against what he described as the "Jewish menace." The most incendiary stories were reprinted into four volumes titled *The International Jew*. My father never drove a Ford. And let us not forget famed aviator and Nazi sympathizer Charles Lindbergh, who achieved international recognition in 1927 after becoming the first person to fly solo and nonstop across the Atlantic Ocean in the plane *Spirit of St. Louis.*

As the Holocaust started in 1933 in Europe, the United States tightened its immigration policies to ensure that Jews trying to escape death in Europe could not emigrate to the United States. The State Department under Franklin Roosevelt was antisemitic, and they used every tool at their disposal to refuse Jews entry into the United States as refugees from Nazi Germany. At the International Evian Conference, which was assembled to discuss the Jewish refugees of the Nazi occupation of Europe, the United States suggested that "no country would be expected or asked to receive a greater number of immigrants than is permitted by its existing legislation."[39] The administration's position was self-serving. America had reformed its immigration laws to limit settlers from any one country not to exceed 3 percent of existing immigrants from that nation already living in the United States. For example, in 1938, the maximum refugee quota was 27,370 from Germany, and only 6,542 from Poland, where 3,300,000 Jews eventually perished in the Holocaust.[40] One of the reasons advanced for this legislation was to limit the influx of Jews.[41] In fact, antisemitism in America was mainstream, and conspiracy theories represented views that Jews were communists and wielded too much political and economic power.[42] Furthermore, opinion polls indicated that one-third of Americans held antisemitic views that in turn affected public policy.[43]

---

[39] Medoff, *supra* note 179, at 6.

[40] *Id.* at 4. *See also, The "Final Solution": Estimated Number of Jews Killed,* Jewish Virtual Library, http://www.jewishvirtuallibrary.org/jsource/Holocaust/killedtable.html (last visited Jan. 22, 2015).

[41] Medoff, *supra* note 179, at 3; *See also,* Feingold, *supra* note 175, 61–62.

[42] Even American hero Charles Lindbergh weighed in on Jewish influence. Breitman and Lichtman, *supra* note 176, 187–88. *See also,* Feingold, *supra* note 175, 196–99; Wyman, *supra* note 178, at 9–15; Medoff, *supra* note 179, at 3 at 2–3.

[43] Medoff, *supra* note 179, at 3; Feingold, *supra* note 175, at 61–62.

For the first five years of the Holocaust, Roosevelt convened 430 press conferences and mentioned the Jewish refugees only one time.[44] Moreover, the administration and Congress refused to alter immigration quotas for fear of too many Jews entering America, or to pressure Britain to change its policies to allow more refugees into Palestine.[45] President Roosevelt's feeble efforts to liberate Jews were highlighted by his refusal to bomb German railways and transit lines, known at the time to be carrying Jews to death camps.[46] In particular, America's tactics to block immigration to the States were underscored by a well-known incident regarding the ship *St. Louis*. This vessel, carrying nine hundred Jewish refugees from Nazi Germany, was denied entry into the United States with the full knowledge of President Roosevelt and State Department officials. The ship eventually had to return to Europe, where many of the passengers eventually were sent to death camps.[47] Additionally, the United States even took steps to deport Jews back to occupied countries because of alleged immigration violations.[48] In a cruel twist of fate, American immigration laws prohibited granting visas for anyone with a

---

[44] Medoff, *supra* note 179, at 5–6.

[45] *Id.* at 10; Wyman, *supra* note 178, at 190.

[46] Feingold, *supra* note 175, at 151. The party line by officials was that a bombing campaign would require resources that would divert from the greater war efforts. For a detailed discussion of the decision to forgo bombing of transit lines to death camps and Auschwitz, see Wyman, *supra* note 178, at 288–307. Furthermore, the World Jewish Congress requested Administration to bomb Auschwitz: *The World Jewish Congress in New York Asks the War Department to Bomb the Crematoria At Auschwitz*, pbs.org, http://www.pbs.org/wgbh/amex/holocaust/filmmore/reference/primary/bombworld.html (last visited Jan. 22, 2015).

[47] *Shoah: Turkey, the US and the UK*, *supra* note 5 at 38–46. The ship originally was originally headed to Cuba, but was denied entry and headed to the United States instead. Feingold, *supra* note 175, at 63, 79.

[48] United States ex rel. Weinberg v. Schlotfeldt, 26. F. Supp. 283 (D. Ill. 1938). The court stated, "Under conditions as they now exist it would be cruel and inhuman punishment to deport this petitioner to Czechoslovakia, belonging as he does to the race which is thus being persecuted and exiled. . . ." *Id.* at 284.

criminal record, which was interpreted to include persons that were in labor or concentration camps.[49] In sum, these intentional and obstructive actions to prevent the rescue of Jews were commonplace and part of a broader strategy of the Roosevelt administration.[50]

It later became public that the State Department was infiltrated with antisemitism at very high levels, and in an internal communication, Assistant Secretary Adolf Berle dictated the tactic to block Jewish immigration into the United States:

> We can delay and effectively stop for a temporary period of indefinite length the number of immigrants into the United States. We could do this by simply advising our Consuls to put every obstacle in the way and to require additional evidence and to resort to various administrative advices which would postpone and postpone and postpone the granting of the visas.[51]

Near the end of the war, Josiah Dubois, a young attorney in the Treasury Department, cataloged the intentional concealment by State and Treasury officials concerning their knowledge of Hitler's "Final Solution." Dubois prepared a memorandum for President Roosevelt entitled, "The Acquiescence of this Government in the Murder of the Jews" and threatened to go to the press.[52] In this detailed document to the president, Dubois wrote, "The tragic history of this Government's

---

[49] *Shoah: Turkey, The US and the UK, supra* note 5, at 12. Another reason advanced for America refusing refugees was the economic factor. The property of Jews had been confiscated in Europe; consequently, many refugees had limited resources. Immigration laws at the time prohibited entry for individuals likely to become a public charge (LPC), and neither the Administration nor Congress was motivated to make exceptions. *Id.*

[50] Wyman, *supra* note 178, at xx–xxi; Feingold, *supra* note 175, at 200.

[51] *An Ambassador and A Mensch, supra* note 8, 172–73; Medoff, *supra* note 179, at 22–23.

[52] See Dubois's full report, handed to Treasury Secretary Henry Morgenthau Jr. for President Roosevelt, in Medoff, *supra* note 179, at 40–52.

handling of this matter reveals that certain State Department officials are guilty of the following: They have not only failed to use Government machinery at their disposal to rescue Jews from Hitler but have even gone so far as to use this Government machinery to prevent the rescue of these Jews.[53] Roosevelt, facing humiliation in an election year, was forced to capitulate. He formed the War Refugee Board,[54] which would operate out of Istanbul to facilitate the immigration of Jewish refugees.

The lessons of the Holocaust are universal. As the United Nations Educational, Scientific and Cultural Organization has described, what happened to the Jewish people in Europe:

- Demonstrates the fragility of all societies and of the institutions that are supposed to protect the security and rights of all. It shows how these institutions can be turned against a segment of society. This emphasizes the need for all, especially those in leadership positions, to reinforce humanistic values that protect and preserve free and just societies.

- Highlights aspects of human behavior that affect all societies, such as the susceptibility to scapegoating and the desire for simple answers to complex problems; the potential for extreme violence and the abuse of power; and the roles that fear, peer pressure, indifference, greed, and resentment can play in social and political relations.

- Demonstrates the dangers of prejudice, discrimination, and dehumanization, be it the antisemitism that fueled the Holocaust or other forms of racism and intolerance.

---

[53] *Id.* at 41.

[54] The War Refugee Board was comprised of officials from the Departments of State, War, and Treasury. Their responsibility was to facilitate the rescue of Jewish refugees, OFER, *supra* note 5, at 269. *See also*, SHOAH: TURKEY, THE US AND THE UK, *supra* note 5, at 179–81; WYMAN, *supra* note 178, at 204–06.

- Deepens reflection about contemporary issues that affect societies around the world, such as the power of extremist ideologies, propaganda, the abuse of official power, and group-targeted hate and violence.

- Teaches about human possibilities in extreme and desperate situations, by considering the actions of perpetrators and victims as well as other people who, due to various motivations, may tolerate, ignore, or act against hatred and violence. This can develop an awareness not only of how hate and violence take hold but also of the power of resistance, resilience, and solidarity in local, national, and global contexts.[55]

Today, we use the Holocaust to remember that we, as world citizens, can and must do better. We all need to fight back against hatred; as Elie Wiesel once famously said, "We must take sides. Neutrality helps the oppressor, never the victim."

Which brings us back to the IHRA definition.

The IHRA definition was developed in 2003–2004 and published in 2005 because with evidence that antisemitism was once again on the rise, experts determined that in order to address the problem of antisemitism, there must be clarity about what antisemitism is. The IHRA definition states: "Antisemitism is a certain perception of Jews, which may be expressed as hatred toward Jews. Rhetorical and physical manifestations of antisemitism are directed toward Jewish or non-Jewish individuals and/or their property, toward Jewish community institutions and religious facilities."

The IHRA definition is important because it derives its power from consensus. It has become the internationally accepted standard definition of antisemitism: It is used by various agencies of the federal government and the thirty-three governments that are members of IHRA, recommended for use by the European Council and the European Parliament,

---

[55] https://en.unesco.org/news/importance-teaching

endorsed by the UN Secretary General and the Secretary General of the OAS, and included in policy guides prepared by the Organization for Security and Cooperation.

In addition, from a domestic perspective, it is particularly important on campus, because in December 2019, President Trump signed a new executive order codifying longstanding Department of Education Office of Civil Rights (OCR) policy that, for the purposes of Title VI discrimination claims, Jewish students are protected against antisemitism, and that when evaluating these claims, the department should consider the IHRA definition. In fact, my firm is currently handling one of the very first cases brought under this new order.

Finally, the Holocaust Remembrance definition is also important on a symbolic level. We cannot let people hide and justify their antisemitism. We need to call it out, and we need to do so in a way that recalls what happens when hatred is left unchecked. We have seen firsthand, in living memory, the dangers of where antisemitism can lead. Six million Jewish people were taken like sheep to the slaughter, and while the murderous Nazis are forever associated with evil, we must also remember the indifference that allowed them to come to power. Using the IHRA definition provides a clear and direct link to why this fight is so important. We can never be indifferent, and as soon as we see a disturbing trend, we must all take a united stand against it.

Unfortunately, we have been seeing such a trend around the world and even here in the United States of America. Data shows that although Jews make up less than 2 percent of the American population, they are among the most likely of all minority groups to be victimized by incidents of hate. The frequency and severity of antisemitic incidents are quickly trending upward. A report issued by the Anti-Defamation League detailed a shocking 67 percent increase in incidents from 2016 to 2017. A 2015 Louis D. Brandeis Center–Trinity College study found that most Jewish American college students had personally experienced or witnessed antisemitism. An AMCHA Initiative survey found a 45 percent increase in antisemitic activity on college and university campuses between 2015 and 2016. More broadly, antisemitic crime and discrimination in the United States has been rising at an alarming rate in recent years, with many tragic events readily testifying to the dangerous level to which this problem has arisen. The shootings at the Tree of Life Synagogue in Pittsburgh, Pennsylvania, in 2018 and at the Chabad of Poway in California in 2019 are recent examples in the United States. A series of random physical attacks throughout 2019 on identifiably Jewish persons in New York City are still present in the minds of many. The ongoing desecration of Jewish cemeteries and vandalism of synagogues with swastikas are more evidence of this growing trend. These examples are easily recognizable as antisemitic activities because they target individuals and institutions on the basis of their apparent Jewish characteristics. Furthermore, the perpetrators of these crimes generally do not pretend to hide the nature of their sentiment toward Jews.

My law practice also involves significant efforts in the area of protecting the First Amendment and free speech, so it is important to make a few things clear. First, I am and always have been a proponent and defender of the First Amendment and freedom of speech. However, the First Amendment does not protect criminal and discriminatory behavior, and it is critical to note that the executive order we are discussing only relates to such activity. It has no effect whatsoever upon the exercise of free speech rights or any other lawful private conduct.

It is also important to point out that the IHRA definition does not suggest, as many claim, that it is inherently antisemitic to criticize Israel. Criticism of Israel is as valid as criticism of any other country in instances where Israel is held to the same standards as other countries. However, criticism of Israel crosses the line into antisemitism when it veers into the realm of demonizing the state or its citizens, or suggesting that it has to behave according to a different set of standards than other states, or that Israel has no right to exist and should be eliminated and its citizens scattered. Nevertheless, even where the most offensive of antisemitic speech is to be found, the First Amendment protects such expression, and the executive order does not challenge that fact. Only when coupled with illicit criminal and/or discriminatory conduct does the definition become relevant, and importantly, the bill does not penalize anything new; it just gives schools a better tool in identifying discriminatory conduct.

As you can probably tell, honoring the memories of the victims of the Holocaust is a force that animates my work and drives me to make sure that we as a society never even come close to heading down that road again. I believe that we all have an obligation to stand up and call out antisemitism when it rears its ugly head, and so I encourage all of you, as members of society, to join me in supporting IHRA.

God is watching.

## ABOUT THE AUTHOR

Stuart Roth serves as senior counsel to the American Center for Law and Justice and the European Center for Law and Justice. Stuart attended law school with ACLJ's chief counsel, Jay Sekulow, and they have practiced law together since 1980. Stuart is a nationally known and recognized constitutional lawyer and has given his legal analysis and commentary on hundreds of national television and radio broadcasts. Stuart has participated in twelve cases that have been argued before the United States Supreme Court, including the landmark decisions in Mergens and Lambs Chapel that altered the landscape of religious liberties litigation. Stuart has also been involved in cases before the European Court of Human Rights and the International Criminal Court. Part of Stuart's work at the ACLJ is defending Jewish students from antisemitic attacks on college campuses.

*Chapter Eight*

# I LIVED UNDER THE OPPRESSION OF APARTHEID IN SOUTH AFRICA, AND ISRAEL IS NOT AN APARTHEID STATE

**by**
**Olga Meshoe Washington**

Imagine having your food served to you on a tin plate and not a normal ceramic one, because of the color of your skin. Imagine having to use the designated, concealed back entrance of a public hospital to be served by a doctor in a designated room, out of sight of other patients of a different race. Those are but two of the many experiences my parents and millions of other black South Africans experienced during apartheid South Africa.

## THE APARTHEID LIE

Over the years, the term "apartheid" has become so synonymous with the State of Israel that it has lost its original meaning: the government regime in South Africa from 1948 to 1994 that segregated and discriminated non-white South African citizens from white South African citizens. This regime was regulated and institutionalized by a system of over

150 codified laws. By law, black people were dispossessed of their lands, homes, and livelihoods, and forcibly relocated to designated, underdeveloped areas. By law, we were prohibited from using the same transportation system, attending the same public schools, or enjoying the same public facilities as white South Africans. By law, we could not move freely within our own country and were not allowed to formally participate in the main economy of the country. We were denied the right to vote and were forbidden from marrying the person we loved if they were of a different racial group.

In addition, black people of different tribes were separated and grouped into mini-homelands to further strip us of our identity as black South Africans. Although I was born in Pretoria, the capital of South Africa, I was not assigned South African citizenship on my birth certificate but that of one of the several homelands established as a farce for black self-governance. Growing up in apartheid South Africa, I was told by white society that as a black person, only certain dreams were available for me to dream: all others were reserved for white people.

The above descriptions of apartheid South African life are the antithesis of Israeli life. In Israel, by law, Israeli Arabs have the same rights as Israeli Jews. They study in the same school system and are treated as equals to all other Israelis in the same hospitals. Israeli Arabs vote, are elected to the Knesset, and have become Supreme Court Justices. Although not required to join the army, some Arab Christian and Muslim citizens of Israel choose to serve in the Israel Defense Forces. Israeli Arabs enjoy the same privilege as other Israelis to earn academic degrees at Israeli universities of their choice. Buses and trains are open to all; they do not have the signs "Jews only" and "Arabs only" to separate commuters as was the case in apartheid South Africa.

Some argue that the nation-state law adopted by the Israeli Knesset on July 18, 2018, which legally enshrines Israel as the nation-state of the Jewish people, confirms Israel's "apartheid" character. Leading Israeli and non-Israeli professors and jurists acknowledge that this law does not contradict existing law. It does not impact or detract from the existing rights to equality and dignity of all Israeli citizens, which remain enshrined and protected in Israel's Basic Law: Human Dignity and Liberty. The nation-state law merely reaffirms Israel's Jewish majority character and underlying Zionistic founding principles—the very reason for its modern creation as the democratic nation-state of the Jewish people.

Israel's Jewish character was recognized and validated by the League of Nations in 1924, by its successor organization the United Nations in 1947, and again on Israel's acceptance as a formal member of the United Nations in 1949. Just as Japan is the homeland of Japanese people and France is the homeland of French people, Israel is the homeland of Jewish people. The existence of these sovereign countries as homes for their respective peoples is not discriminatory in nature. Of all these nations, and so many others in the 193 member states of the United Nations, Israel is the only nation accused of being an apartheid state. This malevolent double standard constitutes antisemitism according to the internationally accepted 2016 International Holocaust Remembrance Association working definition of antisemitism.

Despite being a Jewish state, Israel's population comprises approximately one-quarter Muslims and is the only state in the Middle East in which other religions, such as Christianity, not only coexist with Judaism but are thriving. Israeli Jews themselves are of more than one color; more than half of the Israeli Jewish population are descendants from North African and Middle Eastern lands. Jews from India, China, and South America also call Israel home. Said differently, the majority of Israel's population is non-white.

## THE PEDDLING OF AN ANTISEMITIC LIE

Anti-Zionists often refer to the late former president of my country, Nelson Mandela, as an authoritative validator of the apartheid lie. One of the most-used quotes from Nelson Mandela for this purpose is "We know too well that our [South Africa's] freedom is incomplete without the freedom of the Palestinians," from his speech given on the International

Day of Solidarity with the Palestinian People in 1997. What is not told is that Mr. Mandela visited Israel in 1999, something those who perpetuate the apartheid narrative don't want the world to do. On this visit, Mr. Mandela said, "I cannot conceive of Israel withdrawing if Arab states do not recognize Israel within secure borders." This is a Zionistic statement. While Nelson Mandela was pro-Palestinian, he was not anti-Israel.

In addition to dishonestly misrepresenting the positions of authoritative and respected individuals such as Mr. Mandela to underpin their deceptive narrative, journalists and information sites are often guilty of furthering the apartheid narrative. The Institute for Middle East Understanding (IMEU) presents itself as a resource hub for journalists seeking information on the socioeconomic, political, and cultural aspects of Israel (which it calls "Palestine") and Palestinians, for purposes of educating the general public. IMEU describes Israel as an "occupier" that engages in "ethnic cleansing" in Jerusalem. It also nefariously ascribes Israel's administration of the West Bank, the result of a bilateral diplomatic agreement with the Palestinian Liberation Organization and which was internationally witnessed and guaranteed by the Oslo Interim Accords in 1995, as the basis for Israel being an apartheid state.[56]

It is true that racism exists in Israel. Racism also exists in mature democracies such as the United States and Great Britain. It exists in today's democratic South Africa. If the United States, Great Britain, South Africa, and other countries are not described as apartheid states, it begs the question why is Israel singled out as being an apartheid state because racism can be found within her.

---

[56] The above-mentioned Oslo Interim Accords divided the West Bank into three zones. Depending on the zone, Israel or the Palestinian leadership was assigned all, some, or no civil and security jurisdiction of the zone in question. Not only is it factually incorrect and dishonest to describe Israel's civil and/or security administration of the zones, per the Oslo Accords, as "apartheid," it is a deliberate omission of history.

## A COLONIAL SETTLER STATE?

What of the argument that Israel is a colonial settler state? That question may be answered by another: can a native become a settler?

From as far back as the second millennium BCE, there has always been a significant Jewish presence in the land that comprises the modern state of Israel, Gaza, and the disputed territories of the West Bank. Historical data and archeological artefacts testify to the existence of Jewish culture, politics, and an economy for three thousand years. They demonstrate that Jews are the indigenous people of the land. The immigration of Jews from across the world to the State of Israel does not equate to the increasing occupation of dispossessed land by the dispossessors, but the return of the indigenous people to their homeland. This homeland includes East Jerusalem and West Jerusalem. Indigenous people cannot be settlers. The Jews are not settlers. Israel is not a colonizer.

Calling Israel a colonial settler state is an insult to every African nation that was colonialized. It also dismisses the fact that the economic and political instability that characterizes much of Africa today owes most of its existence to Europe's egregious colonialization of all but two African nations.

## THE TRUE COST OF THE ISRAEL APARTHEID NARRATIVE

Lies empower evil. Lies about blacks empowered apartheid in South Africa. Lies about Jews made the Holocaust possible. With all her imperfections, Israel is not an apartheid state. This false claim masks the true antisemitic intentions of those who call Israel an apartheid state. It has misled many well-intentioned people around the world into opposing the only true democracy in the Middle East. This apartheid lie continues to embolden antisemitic acts on innocent Jews in the privacy of their homes, during their times of worship, and on college campuses. It odiously characterizes non-Jewish Zionists and supporters of Israel as accomplices of Israel's fictitious crimes against humanity. More importantly, it compromises the chances of peace in the Middle East.

Equally important but oftentimes forgotten, the apartheid label assigned to Israel redirects focus away from holding the Palestinian Authority and Hamas accountable for their ill treatment and abuse of the Palestinian people.

## CONCLUSION

Calling Israel an apartheid state trivializes the humiliation and injustices endured by black South Africans who lived through apartheid and who still, together with their children and grandchildren, bear the scars of its legacy. If black South Africans enjoyed the rights enjoyed by Israeli Arabs, there would have been no need for South Africa's liberation movement. There would not have been a Nelson Mandela as the world knows him or other freedom fighters who spent much of their lives incarcerated, and whose families sacrificed much for the democracy South Africa enjoys today.

In addition to being antisemitic, it is morally repugnant for any person, any organization, or any government to incorrectly appropriate South Africa's apartheid history to Israel. It is also repulsive to rally people across the world on the painful, collective, lived experiences of black South Africans for a cause premised on falsehood. Black South Africans must decide that their moral authority on what apartheid is and what it is not cannot be bought; that their history cannot be manipulated to perpetuate a narrative that erases the boundary between legitimate criticism of policies of the Israeli government and antisemitism. It is incumbent upon all persons who genuinely desire to see peace in the Middle East and who have a sincere interest in the liberation of the Palestinian people from their oppressive leaders to seek the truth and speak the truth against a narrative that is core to an agenda to delegitimize, demonize, and ultimately destroy the State of Israel and Jewish life in the diaspora.

## ABOUT THE AUTHOR

Olga Meshoe Washington holds an MBA and is an accomplished lawyer, speaker, and writer. Olga's unique narrative on South African and African relations with Israel, as well as on the Christian mandate to stand with Israel, and her engaging delivery have contributed to Olga being a regular on the speakers' circuit in Africa and the United States. A South African native, Olga is the chief executive officer of Defend Embrace Invest Support Israel (DEISI) International. Olga's courageous support of the Jewish people led *The Times of Israel* to name her "Israel's Warrior." *Parable Magazine* named Olga as one of South Africa's 2011 influential young Christian leaders, and in 2016, she received the 2016 Jerusalem Award from the World Zionist Organization, in recognition of advocacy for the State of Israel and South African Jewish Community.

*Chapter Nine*

# ANTISEMITISM REARS ITS UGLY HEAD AT THE INTERNATIONAL CRIMINAL COURT

by
**Jay Alan Sekulow**
**and Robert Weston Ash**

Modern international law traces its origin to the Treaty of Westphalia in 1648,[57] which ended the bloody Thirty Years' War in Europe and set the foundation for the rules that would henceforth govern relations between and among states. The current international system based on nation-states traces its lineage to that treaty. One of the principles that grew out of the treaty was the concept of the sovereign equality of states. In other words, each state, irrespective of its geographical extent, its economic strength, its population size, or its political system is deemed to be equal with every other state.[58]

---

[57] The Treaty of Westphalia (1648), *available at* https://pages.uoregon.edu/dluebke/301ModernEurope/Treaty%20of%20Westphalia%20%5BExcerpts%5D.pdf.

[58] Note that the Westphalian system was based on Judeo-Christian concepts of law as understood by European states. Initially, the Westphalian order simply regulated relations between and among European states. With the demise of the age of colonialism, newly emerging states were welcomed into the community of nations, and they now enjoy the same rights as the original European states.

Yet, all too often, when it comes to the State of Israel, the only *Jewish* state in the community of nations, this principle—the equality of states—is somehow ignored. Israel is singled out for prejudicial treatment at virtually every international venue, like the United Nations (UN) and its various organs (like the United Nations General Assembly [UNGA], the UN Human Rights Council [HRC], UNESCO, WHO, etc.). Regrettably, the International Criminal Court (ICC) seems intent on joining this infamous list.

In mid-March 2020, lawyers from the European Centre for Law and Justice (ECLJ) had an opportunity to assist Israel at the ICC by submitting an amicus curiae brief to the ICC, disputing the claim by the ICC Office of the Prosecutor (OTP) that it has authority to extend ICC jurisdiction over Israeli nationals with respect to the so-called "Situation in Palestine."[59]

The ICC was envisioned as an institution to investigate, try, and punish persons for the worst atrocities, namely genocide, crimes against humanity, war crimes, and the crime of aggression.[60] Yet, given the genuine large-scale atrocities perpetrated around the world in the last decade alone, it defies belief that the State of Israel should even be on the ICC's radar.[61]

---

[59] Situation in Palestine, Case No. ICC-01/18, Prosecution Request Pursuant to Article 19(3) for a Ruling on the Court's Territorial Jurisdiction in Palestine, paras. 3, 220 (Jan. 22, 2020) [hereinafter Prosecutor's Request], https://www.icc-cpi.int/CourtRecords/CR2020_00161.PDF.

[60] Rome Statute of the International Criminal Court, arts. 1, 5, July 17, 1998 [hereinafter Rome Statute], https://www.icc-cpi.int/resource-library/documents/rs-eng.pdf.

[61] *See*, e.g., "Syria Events of 2018," Human Rights Watch, https://www.hrw.org/world-report/2019/country-chapters/syria (last visited June 9, 2020) (reporting the death toll since the start of the war to be as high as 511,000 as of March 2018 and "6.6 million displaced internally and 5.6 million around the world."); Ben Hubbard, "Dozens Suffocate in Syria as Government Is Accused of Chemical Attack" (Apr. 8, 2018), https://www.nytimes.com/2018/04/08/world/middleeast/syria-chemical-attack-ghouta.html; John Walcott and W.J. Hennigan, *U.S. Spies Say Turkish-Backed Militias Are Killing Civilians as They Clear Kurdish Areas in Syria* (Oct. 28, 2019), https://time.com/5711596/syria-war-crimes/.

Moreover, ICC jurisdiction is meant to be complementary to national criminal jurisdictions.[62] This means that individual states have the primary responsibility to carry out investigations and prosecutions of such crimes, and, as long as a state does so, the ICC may not intervene.[63] Israel is just such a state. It guarantees full and equal rights under the law to all of its citizens—Jews and non-Jews alike. Israel has robust independent legal and judicial institutions. Its military is considered by the militaries of other democracies as a leader in efforts to reduce enemy civilian casualties in military operations.[64] The Israeli military is fully subordinate to the civilian judicial authorities that supervise its adherence to the Law of Armed Conflict (LOAC). There are few, if any, parallels to this anywhere in the world. Israel faces grave threats to its security. It is perpetually under attack by a number of adversaries. It is the only country in the world whose right to exist is constantly questioned and which is regularly threatened with physical destruction.[65] Nevertheless, Israeli authorities investigate complaints regarding alleged violations of the LOAC by Israeli personnel and, when the evidence supports, prosecute members of the armed forces or subject them to administrative disciplinary proceedings. If Israel's legal system doesn't make the cut, it is difficult to imagine a legal system that does.

---

[62] Rome Statute, *supra* note 4, pmbl. and art. 1.

[63] "Complementarity Principle," European Center for Constitutional and Human Rights, https://www.ecchr.eu/en/glossary/complementarity-principle/ (last visited June 4, 2020).

[64] David Alexander, "Israel Tried to Limit Civilian Casualties in Gaza: U.S. Military Chief," *Reuters* (Nov. 6, 2014), https://www.reuters.com/article/us-israel-usa-gaza/israel-tried-to-limit-civilian-casualties-in-gaza-u-s-military-chief-idUSKBN0IQ2LH20141106; High Level Military Group, An Assessment of the 2014 Gaza Conflict (Oct. 2015), *available at* http://www.high-level-military-group.org/pdf/hlmg-assessment-2014-gaza-conflict.pdf.

[65] *See*, e.g., AFP, "Top Iran General Says Destroying Israel 'Achievable Goal,'" VOA, (Sept. 30, 2019), https://www.voanews.com/middle-east/top-iran-general-says-destroying-israel-achievable-goal. "Hezbollah Leader Hassan Nasrallah: Israel Must Be Destroyed," *Jerusalem Post* (May 22, 2020).

Further, because the ICC is the creation of a treaty (the Rome Statute), it must comply with general principles of international law that govern creation of treaties and their reach. One such principle is that "[a] treaty does not create either obligations or rights for a third State without its consent."[66] Israel, having declined to accede to the Rome Statute, is just such a third State vis-à-vis the Rome Statute and the ICC. Yet, despite that well-established customary international law principle, the Rome Statute nonetheless includes a provision that purportedly allows the ICC to try and punish nationals of non-consenting, non-party states like Israel under certain circumstances,[67] and the ICC Prosecutor appears to have her sights set on dragging Israelis into the dock at all costs.

In that regard, on December 20, 2019, the ICC Prosecutor asked an ICC pre-trial chamber (PTC) to rule that the ICC has jurisdiction over crimes committed in the West Bank, East Jerusalem, and the Gaza Strip.[68] She based her request on *her* belief that those territories belong to a "State" of Palestine. Her position is highly problematic, to say the least.

*First*, Israel has been engaged in a longstanding territorial dispute with Palestinian Arabs. Both sides lay claim to the so-called "West Bank," which Israel captured from illegal Jordanian occupation in 1967 after being attacked by Jordan. Israel has administered the territory since then, but its status has never been authoritatively resolved. Israel has a strong

---

[66] Vienna Convention on the Law of Treaties, art. 34, *opened for signature* on May 23, 1969, 1155 U.N.T.S. 331, [hereinafter Vienna Convention].

[67] Rome Statute, *supra* note 4, art. 12(2) (a). Note that the ICC may only exercise authority delegated to it by the States Parties to the treaty that created the court. Israel is not a State Party to that treaty and has not delegated one scintilla of its authority to that court. Note also that, under customary international law, no State Party to that treaty may waive Israel's decision to reject ICC jurisdiction over its territory, nationals, and interests, although that is exactly what the treaty claims the ICC may do.

[68] Prosecutor's Request, *supra* note 3, para. 220.

legal claim to ownership of the territory, but has, to date, refrained from exercising full sovereignty over it, in the expressed hope that the final status of the territory can be settled by negotiation. Several attempts to reach a negotiated settlement have been made, most notably the Oslo Agreements of the mid-nineties, which established limited Palestinian autonomy over parts of the West Bank as a transitional phase towards a final status agreement. The international community has repeatedly and consistently taken the position that the status of the territory must be resolved by negotiations between the parties. Accordingly, *at best*, such territories constitute *disputed* territories whose ownership must be determined via bilateral negotiations between the claimants—the means already explicitly agreed to by both Israelis and Palestinians in a series of agreements between them.[69] No decision on ownership of the territories can legitimately be pronounced by a third party not agreed to by both claimants and not professionally equipped to adjudicate such a dispute (certainly not an ICC panel of judges not recognized by Israel and which, as a criminal court, lacks the capacity and tools to make such a determination).

*Second*, there is not now—nor has there ever been—a Palestinian political entity that meets the recognized criteria under international law for statehood, criteria that the Prosecutor argues should be applied "flexibly" in this case.[70] Hence, she must argue that the disputed territories belong to the fictional "State" of Palestine, because the absence of a "State" of Palestine extinguishes the ICC's ability to exert jurisdiction

---

[69] The PLO and Israel agreed that the "issues that will be negotiated in the permanent status negotiations [are]: Jerusalem, settlements, specified military locations, Palestinian refugees, borders, foreign relations and Israelis." Israeli-Palestinian Interim Agreement on the West Bank and the Gaza Strip, Isr.-PLO, Sep. 28, 1995, art. XVII(1)(a), [hereinafter Oslo II], *available at* https://mfa.gov.il/MFA/ForeignPolicy/Peace/Guide/Pages/THE%20ISRAELI-PALESTINIAN%20INTERIM%20AGREEMENT.aspx.
[70] *See* Prosecutor's Request, *supra* note 3, paras. 137–144.

over Israelis[71] concerning any matters alleged by Palestinians to have taken place in the disputed territories.

Thus, the issue of Palestinian statehood is key. Instead of merely asking the PTC to rule on whether there is, in fact, a "State of Palestine," and if so, what its territorial limits are, the Prosecutor went far beyond what was required by arguing stridently that Palestine should be considered a State "for purposes of the Rome Statute" and asking the Chamber to ratify her view that the West Bank, East Jerusalem, and the Gaza Strip constitute the territories that make up such State.[72] Rather than apply well-established international law criteria to the question at hand, which would be the proper course of action in a proceeding before a court of law, the Prosecutor chose instead to rely on a series of political decisions made by shamelessly biased UN bodies and officials and asked the PTC, in effect, to disregard the law and rely on those same political decisions instead.

The international legal criteria for determining statehood are well established. The Montevideo Convention on the Rights and Duties of States of 1933 (Montevideo Convention) reflects the requirements for statehood under customary international law.[73] Article 1 of the Mon-

---

[71] Because Israel is not a party to the Rome Statute, its refusal to accede constitutes rejection in toto of the terms of that treaty vis-à-vis Israel's territory, its nationals, and its national interests. Thus, under customary international law, Israelis cannot lawfully be subject to the terms of that treaty without the explicit, prior consent of the government of Israel. But, as explained above, article 12(2)(a) of the Rome Statute violates this principle by purportedly allowing the ICC to exercise jurisdiction over a national of a non-party State (like Israel) if such national commits a crime within the jurisdiction of the ICC on the territory of a State Party. If no State of Palestine exists, there is no territorial nexus by which the ICC can ensnare Israeli nationals.

[72] *See,* e.g., Prosecutor's Request, *supra* note 3, para. 43.

[73] *Seventh Int'l Convention of Amer. States, Montevideo Convention on the Rights and Duties of States,* art. 1, Dec. 26, 1933, 165 LNTS 19 [hereinafter *Montevideo Convention*]. *See also* Alexandra Rickart, *Emerging Issues: To Be or Not to Be, That Is the Statehood Question,* 3 Univ. Balt. J. Int'l L. 145, 145 & n.1 (2015) ("[The Montevideo Convention is] considered to be customary international law that applies to all States.").

tevideo Convention established four prerequisites to statehood: (a) a permanent population, (b) a defined territory, (c) a government, and (d) a capacity to enter relations with other States.[74] These four criteria are the prime *indicia* of statehood, and the Palestinian entity's glaring failure to meet these requirements precludes any valid claim to statehood on their part.

Since the ICC is a judicial body, the Prosecutor and the various panels of judges are obligated to apply the Montevideo criteria to determine whether a Palestinian State exists *in fact* under law rather than accept symbolic actions or biased political statements by various UN bodies as a substitute for the law. Had the Prosecutor's office objectively applied the Montevideo criteria, it would have had no alternative but to find that the so-called "State of Palestine" fails that test.

For instance, the claimed "State of Palestine" lacks defined territory. The West Bank, East Jerusalem, and the Gaza Strip are disputed territories. The Palestinian Authority (PA), the political body established for Palestinians to implement the terms of the various accords between Palestinians and Israel, does not have sovereign title or effective control over these territories[75]—and never has. Moreover, both the PA and the Israeli Government have agreed that the issue of "borders" (which is the means used to identify the extent of a State's territory) is to be resolved via negotiations between Palestinian and Israeli officials, certainly not by a third party, let alone a wholly inappropriate forum like the ICC.[76]

Further, the "State of Palestine" does *not* have a government that exercises sovereign control over the territories it claims or the population living there—and never has. This is evidenced by the factional divisions and ongoing disagreements between the PA and Hamas. Hamas

---

[74] Id.

[75] Kavitha Giridhar, Legal Status of Palestine, *available at* https://www.drake.edu/media/departmentsoffices/dussj/2006-2003documents/PalestineGiridhar.pdf.

[76] Oslo II, *supra* note 13, art. XVII(1)(a).

effectively controls the Gaza Strip, while the PA merely exercises limited autonomy over certain areas of the West Bank.[77]

Finally, under the terms of the Oslo Accords, the PA agreed that it does not possess a general capacity to enter into foreign relations—a further requirement for statehood.[78] Specifically, the PA agreed that any dealings between PA officials and foreign officials *"shall not be considered foreign relations."*[79]

Given that the entity known as "Palestine" lacks a defined territory, a functioning government with effective authority over the "territories" it claims, and the ability to enter into foreign relations, no Palestinian "State" exists *in fact.*

The Prosecutor admits as much in her request to the PTC, where she specifically acknowledged 1) that "Palestine does not have full control over the Occupied Palestinian Territory and its borders are disputed" 2) that "[t]he Palestinian Authority does not govern Gaza," and 3) that "the question of Palestine's Statehood under international law does not appear to have been definitively resolved."[80] Yet, incredibly, *notwithstanding these facts,* the Prosecutor asked the PTC to consider Palestine a state for the strict purposes of the Rome Statute, thereby suggesting that,

---

[77] Under Oslo II, the West Bank is divided into three types of Areas, designated A, B, and C. *Id.* art. XI(2). The degree of PA control varies in each area, with the most control in Areas designated A and the least authority in Areas designated C. Even in Areas A, where the PA exercises the most authority, the PA has no control over individual Israelis and does not control airspace or external security. *See* The Israeli-Palestinian Interim Agreement-Annex I, Isr.-PLO, Sep. 28, 1995, arts. V, VIII(1)(a), XIII (4) [hereinafter Oslo II, Annex I], https://mfa.gov.il/MFA/ForeignPolicy/Peace/Guide/Pages/THE%20ISRAELI-PALESTINIAN%20INTERIM%20AGREEMENT%20-%20Annex%20I.aspx. Taken together, Areas A and B constitute approximately 40 percent of the entire West Bank; Areas C constitute the remainder, which remains under near-complete Israeli control. Id. art. V.

[78] *See* Oslo II, *supra* note 13, art. IX(5).

[79] Id. art. IX(5)(b)(4), emphasis added.

[80] Prosecutor's Request, *supra* note 3, at paras. 5, 35.

when it comes to Israel, international law can be either ignored or distorted beyond recognition.

In May 2016, the thirty-one member states of the International Holocaust Remembrance Alliance (IHRA) formally adopted a working definition of antisemitism.[81] As a member of the IHRA, the United States uses this definition, as do the other leading democracies of the world.[82] The guide to the IHRA definition provides various examples of manifestations of antisemitism that include, inter alia, "the targeting of the state of Israel, conceived as a Jewish collectivity," and "*applying double standards by requiring of [Israel] a behavior not expected or demanded of any other democratic nation.*"[83] The notion that, even though Palestine does not meet unambiguous international legal criteria for statehood, it should nonetheless be considered a state for the purposes of the Rome Statute so that Israeli nationals can be hauled before the ICC, is exactly the kind of double standard condemned as antisemitism. No other nation is held to such a skewed standard. The Prosecutor has bent over backwards in singling out Israel. Such treatment of the Jewish State would appear to be a manifestation of antisemitism as defined by the IHRA.

---

[81] "Antisemitism is a certain perception of Jews, which may be expressed as hatred toward Jews. Rhetorical and physical manifestations of antisemitism are directed toward Jewish or non-Jewish individuals and/or their property, toward Jewish community institutions and religious facilities." "Working Definition of Antisemitism," Int'l Holocaust Remembrance Alliance, June 27, 2006 [hereinafter IHRA Definition], available at https://holocaustremembrance.com/stories/working-definition-antisemitism.

[82] "Defining Anti-Semitism," Office of International Religious Freedom, U.S. Dept. of State, https://www.state.gov/defining-anti-semitism/ (last visited May 21, 2020).

[83] IHRA Definition, *supra* note 25. Other examples include, inter alia, "[d]enying the Jewish people their right to self-determination, e.g., by claiming that the existence of a State of Israel is a racist endeavor," "[c]alling for, aiding, or justifying the killing or harming of Jews in the name of a radical ideology or an extremist view of religion," "[a]ccusing Jews as a people responsible for real or imagined wrongdoing committed by a single Jewish person or group, or even for acts committed by non-Jews," etc. Id. (Emphasis added).

This is not the first time that international institutions have disregarded international law when it concerns Israel. This practice is regrettably common among United Nations bodies.[84] But the ICC is a *judicial* body. For a judicial body to disregard clear-cut international law in favor of a contrived novel standard is a greater cause for concern because such actions politicize the legal process and subvert the rule of law. Justice is no longer blind when it applies different strokes to similar folks.

To support her conclusions that Palestine should be considered a state and that the West Bank, East Jerusalem, and the Gaza Strip should be considered Palestinian territories, the Prosecutor relied heavily on nonbinding, political decisions and pronouncements by the UNGA and other UN bodies, including: 1) the change in designation of Palestine by the UNGA from "entity" with observer status to "non-member observer State" status[85]; 2) the claim that the West Bank, East Jerusalem, and the Gaza Strip are "Occupied Palestinian Territories"[86]; 3) the conclusion that the 1949 armistice lines (often referred to today as the "pre-1967 borders") are international borders[87] despite explicit contrary language in the 1949 armistice agreements[88]; and 4) the suggestion that, because the

---

[84] Such as, the UNGA, UNESCO, and Human Rights Council (HRC). "The U.N. and Israel: Key Statistics from UN Watch," UN WATCH, Aug. 23, 2016, https://unwatch.org/un-israel-key-statistics/.

[85] G.A. Res. 67/19, Status of Palestine in the United Nations (29 Nov. 2012), https://undocs.org/A/RES/67/19.

[86] Prosecutor's Request, *supra* note 3, paras. 163–64, 167 (citing UNGA and HRC resolutions that call the disputed territories "Occupied Palestinian Territories").

[87] Id. at para. 193.

[88] *See*, e.g., Israel-Jordan Armistice Agreement, art. IV(2), Israel Ministry of Foreign Affairs, (Apr. 3, 1949), available at https://mfa.gov.il/mfa/foreignpolicy/mfadocuments/yearbook1/pages/israel-jordan%20armistice%20agreement.aspx. ("The basic purpose of the Armistice Demarcation Lines is to delineate the lines beyond which the armed forces of the respective Parties shall not move."): id., art. VI(9) ("The Armistice Demarcation Lines defined in articles V and VI of this Agreement are agreed upon by the Parties *without prejudice to future territorial settlements or boundary lines or to claims of either Party relating thereto.*" [Emphasis added.])

international community, through various UN resolutions, associates the Palestinian people's right to self-determination with the so-called "Occupied Palestinian Territories," we must conclude that those territories are in fact Palestinian territories.[89]

In making such arguments, the ICC Prosecutor has consciously adopted anti-Israel political rhetoric that is commonplace at the UNGA as the "legal rationale" to support her position and has presented such rhetoric as if it were binding law.

The UNGA is a political body composed of all UN Member States. UNGA resolutions reflect member states' political views and opinions, but are not legally binding.[90] The UNGA is anything but an unbiased, objective arbiter of facts. From 2012 through 2017, for example, 75 percent to 85 percent of all UNGA resolutions targeted Israel.[91] Even the globe's worst violators of human rights such as Iran, Syria, North Korea, and Sudan *collectively* did not have that many resolutions against them.[92] Notably, the guide to the IHRA working definition of antisemitism acknowledges that Israel is not immune from legitimate criticism: "criticism of Israel *similar to that leveled against any other country* cannot be regarded as antisemitic."[93] Yet, as the foregoing percentages show, criticism of Israel is not similar to that leveled against any other country.

Instead of recognizing anti-Israel UNGA resolutions as the nonbinding, politically influenced, and frequently antisemitic decisions they are, the Prosecutor chose instead to accord them the force of law. For instance, "armistice lines" are defined as the lines separating hostile forces when hostilities cease. After Israel declared independence in 1948, five

---

[89] Prosecutor's Request, *supra* note 3, para. 193–210.

[90] U.N. Charter, arts. 10–14. Lewis Saideman, "Do Palestinian Refugees Have a Right of Return to Israel? An Examination of the Scope of and Limitations on the Right of Return," 44 Va. J. Int'l L. 829, 835 (2004).

[91] *The U.N. and Israel: Key Statistics from UN Watch*, *supra* note 28.

[92] *See* id.

[93] IHRA Definition, *supra* note 25 (emphasis added).

Arab armies (Egypt, Jordan, Syria, Lebanon, and Iraq) attacked Israel. The fighting ended in 1949 with a series of armistice agreements, which, *at Arab insistence*, designated the lines separating the respective armies as "armistice lines" and specifically refused to acknowledge them as lawful borders.[94] Yet, UNGA resolutions repeatedly and incorrectly refer to the 1949 armistice lines as "pre-1967 *borders.*"[95] For a political body like the UNGA to call armistice lines "borders" is one thing, but for a judicial body like the ICC to simply accept such obviously incorrect legal pronouncements as legally binding decisions is emblematic of the anti-Israel political position of the ICC Prosecutor.

Further, the UNGA position on the disputed territories improperly favors the Palestinian people's aspirations to self-determination, while wholly disregarding the Jewish people's right not only to self-determination but also to defend themselves from attack (for which Israelis are frequently criticized by the ICC Prosecutor[96]). The Prosecutor has taken biased political statements, which call the disputed territories "Occupied Palestinian Territories," and which associate those territories with the Palestinians' right to self-determination, as legally binding conclusions. Instead of analyzing facts on the ground in light of well-established international law, the Prosecutor's office simply adopted such statements as reflecting legal realities without any independent legal analysis.

Additionally, while acknowledging that the PA and Israel have agreements in place that require resolution of final status issues (including borders) via bilateral negotiations,[97] the Prosecutor inexplicably concluded

---

[94] *See*, e.g., Proceedings of the 64th Annual Meeting of the American Society of International Law, 894–96 (1970) (noting that language used in 1949 armistice agreements with Israel regarding armistice lines was "at Arab insistence").

[95] *See*, e.g., Prosecutor's Request, *supra* note 3, para 151 and note 510 (citing to multiple UNGA resolutions).

[96] *See*, e.g., "Statement of the Prosecutor of the International Criminal Court, Fatou Bensouda, regarding the worsening situation in Gaza," (Apr. 8, 2018), https://www.icc-cpi.int/pages/item.aspx?name=180408-otp-stat.

[97] Prosecutor's Request, *supra* note 3, para. 72.

that the ICC's exercise of jurisdiction "in no way affects and is without prejudice to any potential final settlement, including land-swaps, as may be agreed upon by Israel and Palestine."[98] Such an assertion defies logic and is absolutely ludicrous. If the Prosecutor's arguments are accepted by the PTC, it would most certainly prejudice Israel's rights and interests by assuming—*in order to allow the ICC to prosecute Israelis for a host of alleged crimes*—that the land in dispute belongs to the Palestinians. Otherwise, the ICC could not exercise jurisdiction over Israeli nationals for offenses that allegedly occurred in such territory until the issue of ownership is resolved. The Prosecutor's position is devoid of logic, contravenes unambiguous principles of customary international law, and fully vindicates the decision by Israel (shared by the United States) not to join the ICC through fear that it would be treated neither fairly nor equally by that institution. In fact, the Prosecutor's logic in this is so faulty as to raise questions concerning her legal competence, in general, and her ability to properly and impartially carry out her responsibilities as ICC Prosecutor in this matter, in particular.

The ICC, as a judicial body, is required to faithfully and impartially apply international law. Yet the Prosecutor's reliance on political pronouncements by politically biased agencies like the UNGA as binding law eviscerates and makes a mockery of the rule of law. Singling out Israel for such treatment further politicizes the ICC, undermines the international rule of law, and reflects knee-jerk, thinly veiled antisemitism endemic in many international institutions.

In sum, the ICC Prosecutor has violated her responsibilities as an officer of the court. Instead of faithfully and even-handedly applying the law, she has chosen to make an exception regarding the so-called "Situation in Palestine" and place her thumb on the Palestinian side of the scale. While having acknowledged that the question of Palestinian statehood is still unresolved and that both Palestinians and Israelis have mutually agreed upon the means to determine what a future State of

---

[98] Id., para. 192.

Palestine will look like (which explicitly includes determining borders which will define where Palestinian sovereignty will apply), she nonetheless proposes to jettison the law that applies universally to all states and invent a different standard for a case involving Israel. That is wrong. It is ultra vires. It is unethical. And, because in so doing she has singled out the only Jewish State for prejudicial treatment accorded to no other, it falls afoul of the IHRA definition of antisemitism.

The ICC was intended as a noble institution dedicated to the lofty goal of punishing the world's worst wrongdoings. Yet, by disregarding clear-cut international law principles in order to put the Jewish State in the dock, a state demonstrably unsuited to the role of accused at the ICC, the Prosecutor's actions paint the ICC as just another notoriously flawed international institution that fails dismally to live up to the ideals that surrounded its creation. Even as the Prosecutor claims to be seeking lofty goals, she readily resorts to an ends-justify-the-means methodology, which in fact subverts the cause of justice. This is why it is necessary to closely monitor what ICC officials are doing and why we submit periodic legal memoranda pointing out how the ICC's actions are in contravention of customary international law. Continued failure to hearken to non-party states' and NGOs' warnings about ICC legal wrongdoing will be the court's ultimate undoing. Israel is only the first democratic state in the ICC's sights. Non-party states like Israel cannot long tolerate unlawful meddling by ICC bureaucrats and busybodies in their internal affairs. As a non-party state to the Rome Statute, Israel has rejected—as is its right as a sovereign state under customary international law—ICC jurisdiction over its territory, nationals, and national interests. There is still time for the Prosecutor to recognize non-party states' rights under customary international law and end her attempts to unlawfully expand ICC jurisdiction over non-consenting, third-party states' nationals. But the hour is late.

We at the ECLJ stand for the rule of law and are resolved to fight this travesty with all the legal means at our disposal.

# ABOUT THE AUTHORS

Dr. Jay Alan Sekulow is chief counsel at the American Center for Law and Justice (ACLJ), Washington, DC, and at the European Centre for Law and Justice (ECLJ), Strasbourg, France. Dr. Sekulow has presented oral arguments in numerous cases before the Supreme Court of the United States on an array of constitutional issues and has filed several briefs with the Court on issues regarding national security and the law of armed conflict. He has had several landmark cases become part of the legal landscape in the area of religious liberty litigation in the United States. Dr. Sekulow's foreign practice has included arguing before the Appeals Chamber of the International Criminal Court in The Hague. Dr. Sekulow has twice been named one of the "100 Most Influential Lawyers" in the United States by the *National Law Journal* and has been listed as "one of the 90 Greatest Washington Lawyers of the Last 30 years" by the *Legal Times*. Dr. Sekulow serves as a faculty member in the Office of Legal Education for the United States Department of Justice. Dr. Sekulow received his bachelor of arts (BA) degree (*cum laude*) and his juris doctor (JD) degree (*cum laude*) from Mercer University, Macon, Georgia. Dr. Sekulow received his doctor of philosophy (PhD) degree from Regent University. He wrote his dissertation on American legal history and is the author of numerous books, law review articles, and other publications. Dr. Sekulow serves as counsel to the 45th President of the United States.

Mr. Robert W. Ash is senior counsel at the American Center for Law and Justice (ACLJ), Virginia Beach, Virginia, and at the European Centre for Law and Justice (ECLJ), Strasbourg, France. Mr. Ash received his bachelor of science (BS) degree from the United States Military Academy at West Point, New York; his master of international public policy (MIPP) degree from the School of Advanced International Studies (SAIS) of the Johns Hopkins University, Washington, DC; and his juris doctor (JD) degree (cum laude) from the Regent University School of Law, Virginia Beach, Virginia. During his Army career, Mr. Ash was a

George and Carol Olmsted Scholar who studied two years at the University of Zurich, in Zurich, Switzerland. He also served as a congressional fellow for one year in the office of Senator John McCain of Arizona. Mr. Ash has taught international law and national security law courses at the Regent University School of Law, and he currently heads the national security practice of the ACLJ. In this latter capacity, Mr. Ash has appeared before and submitted numerous legal memoranda to various organs of the International Criminal Court in The Hague.

*Chapter Ten*

# THE OBLIGATION OF MEMORY

by

**Marlene Warshawski Yahalom, PhD**

t is a privilege for me, Director of Education of the American Society
for Yad Vashem and a daughter and granddaughter of six Holocaust
survivors, to contribute to the publication of *Casualty of Contempt* to
address the rising tide of antisemitism. We need to draw attention to
the degree and reality of antisemitism. It is on the rise and is part of
a current environment stained with discrimination aimed at other victim groups as well. As one way of response, we can consider applying
important strategies developed in Holocaust education by the International School of Holocaust Studies at Yad Vashem.

We must first ask ourselves—why is it important to remember the
Holocaust? How can we ensure that future generations do not forget the
Holocaust? What advocacy do we owe to Holocaust survivors? What
lessons can we teach and learn from to ensure that manifest and latent
forms of antisemitism are identified and addressed before they develop
and escalate to dangerous proportions?

The Holocaust is not simply a contemporary issue. It stretches back
past the parameters of the modern era—into the medieval age and
beyond to the inception of antisemitism. Antisemitism, discrimination

of Jews of all walks of life, was not a new concept in 1933. It was widespread and prevalent in many countries. The Nazi regime amplified and manipulated the latent prejudices of its citizens. It did not create these prejudices.

The Holocaust also demonstrates the atmosphere in which genocide can take place. The beliefs that result in a genocide survive because the political and social climate makes these beliefs acceptable and unchallenged. The Holocaust, therefore, must be remembered because it is an example of how these trends can and do become more threatening.

The hatred of the Holocaust may be understood as manifestations of historical antisemitism. In the realm of Holocaust education, this hatred persists by Holocaust deniers who question the validity of this event. While as a nation, we advocate freedom of speech and expression, this principle rests on due diligence of fact-checking with regard to the subject matter. Either through ignorance or purpose, antisemitism is taking a new presence in the arena of public opinion. It is apparent in Holocaust denial and in shifting attitudes about Israel.

Our responsibility from the lessons of the Holocaust is to ensure that the representation of history is accurate and true. In doing so, we are mindful of the role of history as a vehicle to transmit the lessons of this event—to treat all people with respect, dignity, and humanity. Practicing due diligence in sustaining accurate information is key. Education is a critical part of this process. By encouraging learning and evaluating facts, we enable communities to make informed decisions guiding their attitudes and choices. Communities with proactive citizens striving for the greater good is a key objective. Holocaust education is a key resource for these messages and lessons.

We are all painfully aware of the challenges we have encountered while executing this mission. These serious challenges include the shrinking Holocaust survivor population and, therefore, direct eyewitness testimony, the rapid growth of Holocaust denial facilitated by the reemergence of white supremacists, and the sheer passage of time since the Holocaust.

Educational strategies are therefore put in place to provide guidance and instruction for clarity and "honest reporting" on facts about the Holocaust. The challenge is to address all efforts whose motives are in deep-rooted antisemitism disguised to promote seemingly independent political issues. Examples include minimizing the Holocaust and claiming it never happened. To address these challenges, we focus on raising awareness about the Holocaust, highlighting its significance in global and Jewish history, and empowering teachers to incorporate this subject into their curricula to raise awareness about this important subject.

The legacy of the Holocaust is acutely relevant to understanding the resurgence of antisemitism. The danger lies in the segment of any population that is not an "expert" on a topic and is easily influenced by those who distort knowledge to gain a following. These similar conditions present situations that are targets for information manipulation.

We need to identify the avenues of knowledge dissemination and work to enforce the accurate presentation of facts from these resources. This effort is intended to create a platform for the public to make informed decisions and formulate opinions based on facts and not propaganda. Attempts to distort and manipulate information on the Holocaust or on attitudes toward Israel in order to generate and encourage antisemitism or anti-Zionism is a call to action to recognize the reality of the world around us—antisemitism is couched under rhetoric that is subtle, insidious, and powerful.

In this regard, college campuses have become centers of anti-Jewish activity, with antisemitism rising among students—a threatening omen for the future. Manifestations of this trend might include the targeting of the State of Israel by making it accountable to criteria not required of any other nation, or by holding the Jews collectively responsible for actions of the State of Israel. This is not to say any country is above criticism. Criticism of Israel similar to that leveled against any other country cannot be targeted as antisemitic. Antisemitism is applying a double standard, raising accusations against Israel that include demonizing Israel and claiming Israel's right to exist is illegal. We need to resist efforts to manipulate and distort history. In this process, we need to be mindful of factors that can influence decision-making and counter these efforts through education.

We further present the Holocaust as a way to restore the humanity of each of the six million Jews murdered in the Holocaust. In doing so, we invite the public to appreciate each victim as a person and not as a statistic. By understanding what was lost rather than how it was lost, we create empathy for the victims by presenting them as people and not numbers on a chart. Building on this empathy, we encourage students to realize the obligation to appreciate differences and be tolerant of all groups and minorities. If we do not teach these lessons, then every minority is at risk to be victimized with potentially unimaginable consequences. In the context of today's current events, we realize this lesson perhaps more than ever before.

Teaching about the Holocaust and commemorating this event is ultimately a tribute to the victims and a responsibility incumbent upon generations following the Holocaust. We want to ensure this kind of event will never repeat itself. Had this awareness existed some seventy-five years ago, the name Auschwitz today would simply be another city on the map of Europe.

## REFERENCES

Dershowitz, A., "Being Part of This People, I Am Part of the Unfolding Mystery." Essay in *I Am Jewish: Personal Reflections Inspired by the Last Words of Daniel Pearl*, edited by Judea Pearl and Ruth Pearl, 117–20. Woodstock, VT: Jewish Lights Publishing, 2004.

Esman, A. R., "Is Ignorance About the Holocaust Connected to Soaring Anti-Semitism?" *The Investigative Project on Terrorism* (2020) June 4, pp. 1–5. https://www.investigativeproject.org/8422

Greenstein, C., and E. Osman, *How Reporting on Anti-Semitism Shapes Public Memory* (2019) Pacific Standard, February 22.

https://psmag.com/social-justice/how-reporting-on-anti-semitism-shapes-public-memory.

Inbari, M., K. Bunim, and M. Byrd, "Why Do Evangelicals Support Israel?" (2020) *Politics and Religion*, January 14: pp. 1–36.

Lovett, I., "Younger Evangelicals Waiver in Support for Israel" (2018) *Wall Street Journal*, June 3.

Tibon, A., "The Battle for Young Evangelical's Views on Israel Could Determine the Future of US Policy" (2018) *Haaretz*, October 19. https://www.haaretz.com/us-news/.premium-battle-over-young-evangelicals-views-on-israel-could-make-the-future-of-u-s-policy-1.6570646

"What Americans Know about the Holocaust" (2020) Pew Research Center, January 22. https://www.pewforum.org/2020/01/22/What-Americans-know-About-the-Holocaust

"Working Definition of Anti-Semitism" https://www.holocaustremembrance.com/working-definition-antisemitism

Wren, A., "Meet the Group Trying to Change Evangelical Minds about Israel" https://www.politico.com/magazine/story/2019/03/10/evangelicals-israel-palestinians-telos-225704

## ABOUT THE AUTHOR

Marlene Warshawski Yahalom, PhD, is the Director of Education for the American Society for Yad Vashem. She is responsible for educational outreach and programs, professional development, teacher training, student programming, traveling exhibitions created by Yad Vashem, and community engagement to raise the public's awareness of the lessons of the Holocaust.

She also serves on the Education Advisory Board of the Rose and Sigmund Strochlitz Holocaust Resource Center of the Jewish Federation of Eastern Connecticut and the Advisory Board of *PRISM: An Interdisciplinary Journal for Holocaust Educators*. Dr. Yahalom earned her PhD in Sociology from Columbia University and wrote her thesis on "The Role of Archives in Remembering the Holocaust: a Study in Collective Memory." She also taught courses on the Holocaust: *History and Collective Memory of the Holocaust*, and *Holocaust, Law and Human Rights*. Dr. Yahalom is the daughter and granddaughter of six Holocaust survivors.

# Chapter Eleven

# THE IDEA THAT INSPIRED THE HOLOCAUST HAS BEEN REBORN[99]

**by**

**Aaron David Fruh**

On April 27, 2019, an evangelical nineteen-year-old nursing student named John Earnest armed himself with an assault rifle and drove to a synagogue in San Diego, California, on a crusade to murder Jews. He was motivated by an age-long idea—an idea that led baptized Christians throughout the ages to persecute and murder their Jewish elder brothers and sisters. It was this same idea that led German Christians to commit genocide against their Jewish neighbors. One of the final things John Earnest did before leaving his parents' home to drive to the Poway Synagogue was to post his manifesto on 8chan—an imageboard website that appeals to an internet subculture given to conspiracy theories and, among other things, hatred of Jews. Earnest's four-thousand-word treatise bolsters his claim of a deep Christian faith and draws from a myriad of biblical references providing evidence he retains a significant

---

[99] Portions of this chapter appeared in the May 20, 2019, edition of *The Jerusalem Post* in an article by Aaron David Fruh entitled "First They Came for the Rabbis."

theological framework (though tragically misguided). The manifesto reads like an anti-Judaic religious proclamation from the Middle Ages.

Earnest dredges up one of the Church's oldest antisemitic myths (the blood libel) in his reference to Simon of Trent, a child in Trent, Italy, whose death was falsely blamed on Jews who needed his blood for Passover. Earnest says of Trent, "You are not forgotten Simon of Trent, the horror that you and countless children have endured at the hands of the Jews will never be forgiven." Earnest blames the Jews for controlling the media, the world's banking system, and the porn industry. In reading Earnest's manifesto, you quickly realize there is nothing new to his antisemitism. He's simply an unimaginative hater who drinks from an ancient poisoned well.

The question is, why did John Earnest target a synagogue? Why did he shoot an innocent rabbi along with a sixty-year-old caring woman, Lori Gilbert-Kaye, who lovingly carried out mitzvahs (good deeds) in her community and stood between Earnest's assault rifle and her wounded rabbi, Yisroel Goldstein—losing her life as a result? Why did Earnest shoot an eight-year-old little girl, Noya Dahan, and a thirty-four-year-old visitor from Israel, Almog Peretz, who just wanted to worship the God of Abraham on Passover? If Earnest was so filled with hate over his deepest convictions that Jews greedily control the world's wealth, the media, and the porn industry—why didn't his journey take him to Wall Street or a newsroom or Hollywood? Why a synagogue? Why shoot Rabbi Goldstein and other Jewish worshipers? The answer to this question is troubling.

Though John Earnest firmly believes his actions were born out of his Christian faith, that notion would be impossible because you cannot be filled with hate and be a Christian at the same time. However, one thing is for sure: Earnest murdered because of a religious conviction. The seventeenth-century thinker Blaise Pascal wrote, "Men never do evil so completely and cheerfully as when they do it from a religious conviction." He was right, of course. This "cheerful evil" has never been played out with as much fervent religious conviction as it has against Jews. The fact that John Earnest drew from historical religious anti-Judaism with such precision and forethought in his manifesto should give us all pause. The fact that he was nurtured in a conservative Presbyterian church, and by all accounts faithful with his family in attendance—his father serving as an elder—raises the question of how he came to a conclusion killing Jews was an act of righteousness.

The roots of religious anti-Judaism run deep. By the second century, the early church fathers were passionately distancing themselves from the Jewish roots of the Christian faith. Seething with jealousy, many of these leaders proclaimed the unbiblical notion that the God of Abraham had rejected the Jewish people and transferred all of His promises to Christians. This idea became known as replacement theology (the church has replaced Israel) or supersessionism (the church has superseded Israel). If you place the statements of the more viciously antisemitic church fathers alongside John Earnest's manifesto, you will be hard-pressed to decide which is more hostile.

**John Chrysostom** wrote that the Jews

sacrificed their sons and daughters to devils. . . . They become worse than the wild beasts, and for no reason at all, with their own hands, they murder their offspring, to worship the avenging devils who are the foes of our life. . . . The synagogues of the Jews are the homes of idolatry and devils. . . . They are worse even than heathen circuses. . . . I hate the Jews for they have the law and insult it.[100]

**Peter the Venerable** proclaimed,

Truly I doubt whether a Jew can be really human. . . . I lead out from its den a monstrous animal, and show it as a laughing

---

[100] J. Parkes, *The Conflict of the Church and the Synagogue* (New York: Atheneum, 1969), 100.

stock in the amphitheater of the world, in the sight of all people. I bring thee forward, thou Jew, thou brute beast.[101]

**Martin Luther,** not an early church father but one of the more influential leaders in church history, had this to say in his 1543 treatise, *The Jews and Their Lies*:

> First, their synagogues should be set on fire, and whatever does not burn up should be spread over with dirt. . . . Secondly, their homes should likewise be broken down and destroyed. . . . Thirdly, they should be deprived of their prayer books and Talmuds in which such idolatry, lies, cursing, and blasphemy are taught. . . . Fourthly, their rabbis must be forbidden under threat of death to teach any more. . . . Even if they were punished in the most gruesome manner that the streets ran with their blood, that their dead would be counted, not in the hundred thousand, but in the millions, still they must insist on being right.[102]

Not surprisingly, John Earnest mentions Martin Luther in his manifesto as one of his inspirational mentors.

As replacement theology spread across the pulpits of Christian Europe, the end result was inevitably an attack on synagogues. One example is Rosh Hashanah 1553, when an edict spread throughout Italy that the Talmud and other Jewish texts should be confiscated from synagogues and burned. The idea was that if the wisdom of the rabbis could be destroyed, then the Jews would readily disavow Judaism and accept Christianity.

On the Night of the Broken Glass (Kristallnacht), November 9, 1938, the Nazis, main objective was not merely to vandalize Jewish shops

---

[101] Michael L. Brown, *Our Hands are Stained with Blood* (Shippensburg, PA: Destiny Image Publishers, 1992), 12–13.

[102] Martin Luther, *The Jews and Their Lies* (1543), (Reprinted in York, SC: Liberty Bell Publications, 2004), 37–38.

and businesses but to destroy Judaism. Tyrannical bands of Nazi rioters broke through the doors of synagogues across Germany, Austria, and the Sudetenland, carried out Torah scrolls and Jewish wisdom books, and burned them in the streets. Next, they lit the synagogues on fire, and when the night was over, 267 synagogues were destroyed. In many instances, German city officials mandated the swift demolition of the Jewish houses of worship, billing the Jews for the cost of the removal of the burned debris.

More recent attacks against synagogues include the horrific Pittsburg Tree of Life massacre on October 27, 2018, that claimed eleven lives. On April 11, 2002, a suicide bomber entered the Ghriba synagogue on the island of Djerba in Tunisia and killed twenty-one people. On November 15, 2003, car bombs shattered two synagogues in Istanbul, Neve Shalom, and Beth Israel, taking the lives of thirty people and injuring three hundred. On November 18, 2014, two Palestinian terrorists entered a synagogue in Jerusalem and murdered four Jewish worshipers and a Druze policeman. In Denmark, on February 14, 2015, a Jewish guard was murdered outside of a synagogue where Jewish families were celebrating a bar mitzvah.

What is so alarming about the Poway Synagogue shooting is that it deeply mirrors an ancient and dark religious antisemitism. In his manifesto, John Earnest sees himself as a soldier fighting a religious war to save Christianity from being plundered by Judaism. He states that his Christian faith is his inspiration to murder Jews "for the persecution of Christians of old . . . and the Palestinian Christians" of today. He calls on religious haters like himself to fight a spiritual war against the Jews, "To my brothers in Christ. . . . Be strong. Although the Jew who is inspired by demons and Satan will attempt to corrupt your soul with the sin and perversion he spews, remember that you are secure in Christ." Earnest mixes false Christian piety with a violent political ideology. Another leader Earnest says motivated his hatred also merged religious piety with a murderous ideology against the synagogue. This mentor of Earnest said, "Today, I believe I am acting in accordance with the will of the

Almighty Creator. By defending myself against the Jew, I am fighting for the work of the Lord."[103] His name? Adolf Hitler.

There are many contemporary sources young John Earnest could have drawn from that would have affirmed his religious conviction of anti-Judaism. An internet phenomenon that has a large following, especially among young men, E. Michael Jones portrays himself as a devout Christian who has a moral obligation to oppose Jews. For the Church to heal the social complexities of the world, Jones encourages her to "work for the conversion of the group that is responsible for virtually every social ill in our day—from wars in the Middle East to pornography and gay marriage at home—namely the Jews, around whose evil machinations the axis of history turns. If the Church wants to have its history back, then it will have to contend with the Jews once again as the Apostles and the Church Fathers did 2,000 years ago."

Another frightening antisemite driven by religious conviction is the comedian Owen Benjamin. Owen appeared twice on the Jay Leno show and also on a production of Comedy Central. Sadly, his penchant for the hilarious has strangely gone missing. Watching his hate-filled antisemitic rants on YouTube is a journey into the surreal. Remarkably, like E. Michael Jones, Owen claims a deep devotion to Christ. His YouTube channel has 250,000 followers, and his Twitter, Facebook, and Instagram platforms tens of thousands. He regularly blames Jews for all of the world's social problems—from Hollywood pedophilia to the opioid crisis. He consistently mocks Holocaust victims and proclaims Jews are in alliance with Satan to control the world's banks, Israeli Jews suck the world dry of wealth, and Jewish wisdom books are pure evil. In a recent post, Benjamin calls for violent aggression against Jews: "I will flip over their little coin-counting tables. That's the thing you are supposed to do. Jesus gave us a blueprint. Flip their tables! You say, 'Jesus was a pacifist.'

---

[103] Adolf Hitler, *Mein Kampf* (New York: Houghton Mifflin. London: Hutchinson Publ. Ltd., 1969), 60.

F--- that! He was flipping tables. Dude! Like, you can count your coins now, Jews."

It is uncomfortable to read the statements of antisemitic church fathers; manifestos like John Earnest's, or books and posts by men like E. Michael Jones and Owen Benjamin, who write and speak from a Christian perspective. We want to simply declare these antisemitic views to be un-Christian, thereby conveniently avoiding the issue altogether. But pious Christian men filled with prejudice have devised many evil schemes in the name of religion. Consider the Crusades, inquisitions, and apartheid. As well, though troubling to accept, the Holocaust didn't happen in a vacuum. Hitler didn't act alone. After centuries of replacement theology, German Christians, for the most part, shared Hitler's antisemitism, and many became willing executioners. By detaching Christianity from crimes we deem as un-Christian, we conveniently create a Christianity that is above and detached from history. One Christian leader unwilling to do this was German theologian Martin Niemöller. After the Holocaust, during a lecture in Zurich in 1946, Niemöller stated,

> Christianity in Germany bears a greater responsibility before God than the National Socialists, the SS, and the Gestapo. We ought to have recognized the Lord Jesus in the brother who suffered and was persecuted despite him being . . . a Jew . . . Are not we Christians much more to blame, am I not much more guilty, than many who bathed their hands in blood?

In his book *The Crucifixion of the Jews*, the late Reverend Franklin H. Littell calls into question Christianity's avoidance of the subject of the Holocaust:

> The Holocaust is the unfinished business of the Christian churches, the running sore unattended by its leaders and weakening to its constituents. The most important event in recent generations of church history, it is still virtually ignored in church

school lessons and carefully avoided by preachers in their pulpits. More than anything else that has happened since the fourth century, it has called into question the integrity of the Christian people and confronted them with an acute identity crisis. They have not yet re-established their right to a blessing and a name.[104]

For the most part, replacement theology thankfully died off after the Holocaust when theologians realized it was this very theological framework—driven by contempt and jealousy—that led German baptized Christians to murder six million innocent Jewish men, women, and children. Tragically, replacement theology has made a breathtaking comeback in the last twenty years. Many American Christian leaders are avoiding the lessons of history and fanning the flames of antisemitism.

George Santayana said, "Those who cannot learn from history are doomed to repeat it." George Bernard Shaw said, "We learn from history that we learn nothing from history." In his poem, "The Gods of the Copybook Headings," Rudyard Kipling said, "As it will be in the future, it was at the birth of man. There are only four things certain since social progress began. That the dog returns to his vomit and the sow returns to her mire. And the burnt fool's bandaged finger goes wobbling back to the fire."

Dr. Gary Burge is a leading replacement theologian and teaches New Testament theology at a major evangelical college. In his book *Whose Land? Whose Promise?*, Dr. Burge plunges the reader into the abyss of replacement theology. Shockingly, the book, filled with bias against the Jewish people, numerous factual and egregious errors, misstatements, omissions, and distortions, won the Award of Merit from the voice of evangelicalism—*Christianity Today*. Burge dismisses the Abrahamic covenant God made with Israel and declares that the Jewish people have forfeited God's covenant promises and lost their eternal right to the land

---

[104] Franklin H. Littell, *The Crucifixion of the Jews* (Macon, GA: Mercer University Press, 1986, 1996), 129.

of Israel. Based on his interpretation of John 15, if Israeli Jews do not convert to Christianity, they must be expelled from the land of Israel:

The people of Israel cannot claim to be planted as vines in the land; they cannot be rooted in the vineyard unless first they are grafted into Jesus. Branches that attempt living in the land, the vineyard, which refuse to be attached to Jesus, will be cast out and burned.[105]

Does this line sound familiar? This could be a quote from any anti-semitic tirade from John Chrysostom's to Martin Luther's. If Israeli Jews do not convert to Christianity, are they (according to Dr. Burge's use of John 15:6) to be cast into the flames and burned? What is so concerning about Dr. Burge's use of John 15:6 is that this same Scripture was used during the Spanish Inquisition to justify driving Jews from their homes and land and then burning them at the stake. Rather than being embarrassed over the perversion of John 15:6 by the inquisitors, Dr. Burge unashamedly applies it to the expulsion of Jews from their homes once again. If a passage like John 15:6 has been historically misinterpreted by inhumane and depraved baptized Christian antisemites, why would someone use the same passage to deny Jews the right to their own land today? That an evangelical New Testament professor would call for the "burning" of Israeli Jews if they fail to convert to Christianity is frightening. Yes, Dr. Burge is using a biblical metaphor to strengthen his point, but after the burning and gassing of millions of Jews during the Holocaust, this harsh language is caustic and more than insensitive. These same words have been used over the centuries by Christian leaders to drive Jews out of their communities. Actually, a pogrom (the ransacking of Jewish villages that ended in expulsion) was a preferable penalty for refusing baptism. Often, a failure to convert to Christianity

---

[105] Gary M. Burge, *Whose Land? Whose Promise?* (Cleveland, OH: The Pilgrim Press, 2003), 176.

was punishable by death through burning. When Christian leaders begin to use metaphorical words like "burning" in describing just punishment against Jews who do not convert to Christianity, it is not long before the metaphor becomes reality. The fact that a book of this nature won the Award of Merit from the flagship publication of evangelicalism—*Christianity Today*—speaks volumes about the contempt American Christianity is developing towards Israel.

American Christianity is following the same pathway of contempt toward Israel and the Jewish people as its counterpart in the UK. In her book *Londonistan*, British journalist Melanie Phillips writes about the devastating anti-Israel bias within the Church of England:

> The real motor behind the Church's engine of Israeli delegitimization is theology—or, to be more precise, the resurgence of a particular theology that had long been officially consigned to ignominy. This is "replacement theology," sometimes known also as "supercessionism," a doctrine going back to the early Church Fathers and stating that all God's promises to the Jews—including the land of Israel—were forfeit because the Jews had denied the divinity of Christ. This doctrine lay behind centuries of Christian anti-Jewish hatred until the Holocaust drove it underground. . . . Moreover, replacement theology is not just a form of anti-Zionism; it directly attacks Jewish religion, history, and identity. . . . According to Canon Andrew White, replacement theology is dominant in the Church of England and present in almost every church, fueling the venom against Israel. Lord Carey agrees that replacement theology is the most important driver behind the Church's hatred of Israel.[106]

[106] Melanie Phillips, *Loindonistan* (New York: Encounter Books, 2006), 152, 155.

On the National Day of Prayer a few days after the Poway Synagogue shooting, Rabbi Yisroel Goldstein spoke in a Rose Garden ceremony at the White House. Bandaged and bearing the wounds of the
assault, Rabbi Goldstein explained what he experienced when John
Earnest confronted him with an assault rifle: "I faced evil and the
worst darkness of all time right in our own house of worship." Similar
words were expressed in a press release made by John Earnest's family soon after the attack, "He (our son John Earnest) has killed and
injured the faithful who were gathered in a sacred place on a sacred
day. To our great shame, he is now part of the history of evil that has
been perpetrated on Jewish people for centuries." The "worst darkness
of all time" and the "history of evil perpetrated on Jewish people for
centuries" concern what Pascal was referring to in saying, "Men never
do evil so completely and cheerfully as when they do it from a religious
conviction." The truth that true Christians need to come to grips with
is that the evil of replacement theology is what has led to the historic
persecution of the synagogue and the Jews. Christians must heed God's
promise in Genesis 12:3 to Abraham and his Jewish bloodline: "I will
curse those who curse you" (GNT). In the Hebrew language, God is
making it clear that whoever curses (the Hebrew word, *kilel*, which
means "to show contempt, despise, look down upon, or have a low
opinion of") the Jewish people and the nation of Israel, God Himself
will curse (the Hebrew word, *arar*, which means "to bring to a place of
fruitlessness and powerlessness—to cause to whither"). There is great
casualty in showing contempt toward Israel and the Jewish people. The
church and the nations have suffered incalculable loss because of their
historical persecution of the Jews. A church or Christian denomination
that holds contempt toward Israel will become fruitless and powerless.
History bears this out. The German evangelical church was the stron-
gest in the world prior to World War II. Sadly, not heeding the early
warning signs of antisemitism, the life of German Christianity was
choked out and became, for the most part, fruitless. American mainline
Christianity has already followed in the tragic path of the Church of

England in its contempt toward Israel, and evangelicalism is not far behind. Again, quoting from Franklin H. Littell's book *The Crucifixion of the Jews*:

> A rise of antisemitism is often the first seismographic reading on a serious shift and shearing along the fault lines of bedrock Christianity. The fundamental fault line of false teaching about the Jewish people, antisemitism serves a useful purpose to individuals insecure in their personal identity and to groups uncertain of their present and future prospects. It is therefore indicative of a broader and deeper malaise in the society. . . . The rise of modern political antisemitism in the last century is thus a measure of the churches' failure to minister as well as to teach truthfully about the Jews. Not only the blood of the Jews but the blood of ill-trained and ill-served apostates must therefore be charged to the current account of Christendom. . . . The antisemite is a criminal in his heart and a coward in his public conduct. . . . Toward the helpless which in Christendom has usually meant the Jews, he directs a veritable torrent of contempt, hatred and – when permitted – violence.[107]

So, why did John Earnest attack a synagogue? Because antisemitism that is born out of a religious conviction is rooted in jealousy. Historically, the religious antisemite has been jealous over the chosenness of the Jewish people. If he can delegitimize and dehumanize the Jews, he then can take their calling and chosenness as his own, thereby replacing them. He is filled with contempt for the Jewish people because they have a historical identity. The religious antisemite derives his identity from his hatred of the Jews. Catholic Bishop Edward Flannery has rightly said, "It was Judaism that brought the concept of a God-given universal moral law into the world. The Jews carry the burden of God in history, and for this have never been forgiven."

---

[107] Littell, *The Crucifixion of the Jews*, 109–111.

So, the attack on synagogues, the burning of Torah scrolls and wisdom books, and the attempts to erase not only Judaism but Jews from the world are ultimately aggressions against the God of the Jews. This is why Jews speak of those who die at the hands of antisemites as "kiddush hashem"—ones who sanctify God's name. Amazingly, after centuries of pogroms, relentless persecution, and genocidal aggression against them, the Jewish people still remain. They remain because they have a rendezvous with a destiny given to them by the God of Abraham, who identifies Himself as the God of Israel. It might be time for Christianity in many contemporary circles to celebrate and honor Jewish destiny rather than replace it with their own by embracing and promoting the idea of replacement theology—an idea that has historically led to Christian violence against Jews. If American Christianity continues on her present course of embracing the contempt behind anti-Israelism and anti-Judaism, it will soon become another fruitless and powerless casualty in the church's long history of antisemitism.

## ABOUT THE AUTHOR

Aaron David Fruh is the president of Israel Team Advocates International, whose mission is to communicate the biblical relationship of Christians, Jews, and the State of Israel to students on college campuses. Aaron hosts a weekly radio program on the American Family Radio National Network entitled *Israel and You*, where he discusses topics including the Jewish roots of Christianity and the rise of global antisemitism. Aaron has authored three books: *The Decree of Esther* (Chosen Books), *The Forgotten Blessing* (Chosen Books), and *Bounce* (Baker Books). Aaron coauthored *Two Minute Warning: Why it's Time to Honor Jewish People Before the Clock Runs Out* (Deep River Books) with Coach Bill McCartney, former head football coach at the University of Colorado Boulder. Aaron is a regular contributing writer for *The Jerusalem Post*, where he discusses the resurgence of antisemitic replacement theology within American Christianity. Aaron holds a master's degree from Wheaton College Graduate School in Wheaton, Illinois.

*Chapter Twelve*

# WHY I CHANGED MY MIND ON THE PEOPLE AND LAND OF ISRAEL[108]

**by**

**Gerald R. McDermott, PhD**

I used to be a supersessionist. In fact, for most of my adult life, I believed that after Jesus, God transferred the covenant from Jewish Israel to the New Israel of the church because most of Jewish Israel rejected Jesus as Messiah. I read the parable of the tenants in Matthew 21 that way: the vineyard owner let out his vineyard to new tenants, Gentiles in the church, after the wicked tenants beat, killed, and stoned his servants, and finally his own son.

I believed that the New Testament changed everything about the covenant: God had originally made it with Abraham and his Jewish progeny, focused on this particular people and its particular land, that tiny strip on the eastern Mediterranean the size of New Jersey. But Jesus came to universalize the particular: he extended the Kingdom from being about one people to all peoples, and one from one little land to the whole world.

---

[108] This chapter is adapted from a speech given at a Christ at the Checkpoint conference in Oklahoma City in 2018. https://juicyecumenism.com/2018/10/18/land-of-israel/

While the Old Testament put the Kingdom in physical terms, the New Testament transformed the physical into the spiritual.

As a result, true Israel is no more Jewish Israel but simply the church, which has accepted Jesus, Gentiles, and Jews alike. Because of Jesus, there are no more distinctions between Jews and Gentiles; the Jewish people, apart from Jesus, are of no particular interest to God anymore. And the land of Israel is of no more importance to God than the land of Thailand.

But then I had a wake-up call that started me questioning all these presumptions. I started seeing things in the New Testament that conflicted with this elegant picture.

For example, Romans 11:28–29 was a passage that had been largely ignored by the church until after the Holocaust. Then scholars and theologians started asking, What did we miss that allowed this to happen in what was perhaps the most Christianized country in history? Both Protestant and Catholic scholars agreed they had missed the plain statement by Paul that God still loves the Jewish people, even those who reject Jesus, and that his covenant with Jewish Israel is still in place: Paul says there that his Jewish brothers who reject Jesus as Messiah are "enemies of the gospel, but *are* beloved for the sake of their forefathers, for the gifts and calling of God are irrevocable" (paraphrased and emphasis added). That is, their calling to be God's chosen people is still in place, even at this point late in Paul's career, in Paul's most mature reflection on Jews and Gentiles.

Does Paul mean here merely that Jews have a historic honor? That would suggest that God's covenant *was* in place but is no longer. No, Paul most clearly uses the present tense: *are beloved*. Besides, just a few chapters before this, he suggested the same thing, that his "kinsmen according to the flesh . . . to *them* belong [again, present tense] the adoption, the glory, the covenants . . . and the promises" (Romans 9:3–4, emphasis added).

But, you say, they were Paul's enemy! Even Paul says so. You're right. But Paul also says they were God's and his *beloved* enemy.

But . . . they had been unfaithful to God! They had failed the terms of the covenant again and again, and most recently, by rejecting the Messiah!

Yes, true. But notice that Paul believed the same and yet insists that does not mean they are no longer in the covenant: "What if some were unfaithful? Does their faithlessness nullify the faithfulness of God? By no means! Let God be true, even if everyone is a liar" (Romans 3:3–4).

Later in this letter, Paul says that God purposely hardened the Jews who rejected Jesus, purposely closed their eyes (Romans 11:25), and yet . . . when there is a remnant that *does* accept Jesus, that remnant is a small piece from the whole lump of dough that is Jewish Israel. Not only is "the part of the dough" that accepts Jesus "holy," but "the whole batch is holy" (Romans 11:16).

But you might say you don't understand. Today's Israel is almost entirely secular and is the farthest cry from biblical Israel, which at least was religious—even if the wrong version of religious.

My Jewish Israeli friends tell me that there is spiritual renewal going on in Israel from the top to the bottom of society, but that it is under the radar. It will never be on CNN. Israelis are seeking the God of Israel, unbeknownst to most of the rest of the world.

But you might say, even if that were true, it does not matter. Because Paul says in Galatians 3:28 that because of Christ, there is neither Gentile nor Jew anymore. All are one in Christ Jesus, and there are to be no more distinctions, certainly not ethnic distinctions.

After many years believing this line, I started to realize there is a problem with it. For Paul also says in this verse that in Christ, there is neither male nor female. And he made clear distinctions between male and female roles in church and home, as did Peter. They wrote that wives are supposed to submit to husbands, but they never asked husbands to submit to wives (Ephesians 5:22–24; Colossians 3:18; 1 Peter 3:1). We can disagree with one another on how to *interpret* these household codes, but the mere fact that we disagree shows that there are, in the plain sense of the text, male-female differences that have to be dealt with.

So, if after Jesus, there are no more distinctions between Jews and Gentiles, why does Paul seem to persist in discussing male-female differences?

After getting stuck on these sorts of problems, I took another look at the Matthew 21 parable of the wicked tenants that seemed to justify the idea that God transferred the covenant from Jewish Israel to the mostly Gentile church. On a closer look, it became apparent that the servants the vineyard owner sent were Jewish prophets! And the new tenants were not Gentiles, but the Jewish apostles whom Jesus had elsewhere indicated would head up the reconstitution of the twelve tribes of Israel. For the same, Matthew says that the apostles will one day rule the twelve tribes of Israel (Matthew 19:28). E. P. Sanders, the distinguished New Testament scholar, wrote that these passages imply that the early church believed in a future restoration of Israel. So, there is no transfer from Jews to Gentiles here in Matthew 21 but a transfer from wicked Jews to faithful Jews.

But these passages are just the tip of the iceberg. Jesus had other things to say about future distinctions between Jews and Gentiles. For example, he said that someday in the future, the Jews of Jerusalem will welcome him (Luke 13:35).

But it's not just Jesus in the New Testament. Paul also believes that Jews and Israel will have a distinct future, even while the gospel goes out to the Gentile nations. He says in Romans 11 that after the fullness of the Gentiles has come in, then "all Israel will be saved" (v. 26).

Is this "all Israel" a mixed church of Jews and Gentiles? It does not appear to be. In the same chapter, he identifies this same Israel as Zion and Jacob. Earlier in this chapter, he refers to "my fellow Jews" (v. 14) as the Israel that failed to obtain what it was seeking (v. 7). The subject of all of chapter 11 is clearly Jews in Jewish Israel.

So I started to realize that while the coming of the Messiah has changed everything related to salvation, it has not changed the distinction between men and women; neither has it changed the distinction between Israel and the rest of the world, or between Jews and Gentiles.

It is noteworthy that we continue to see these distinctions in Romans, Paul's most mature theology, written close to the end of his life. Even here, where I had previously thought all Jewish distinctions and advantages for Jews had been abolished, surprisingly they were still present: "Circumcision is of value if you obey the law" (and Paul suggested it is possible to obey the law at one level: he says he was "blameless" in regards to "righteousness under the law" in Philippians 3:6*)*, and "being a Jew" is an "advantage," "much in every way" (Romans 2:25; 3:1–2)!

But I had a hard time accepting this. Isn't this Jewish exceptionalism? Is God giving here special privileges to Jews?

Yes and no. Yes, insofar as *they* were given the burden of chosenness and not the Egyptians or the Canaanites. They had a special covenant and worship, which gave privileges, but also discipline and painful exile when they broke the terms of the covenant.

But no, insofar as Jews and Gentiles alike must come to the Father through the Son—the Jewish Messiah. Being Jewish does not make them automatically saved. As Paul said, many are *in Israel but not of Israel* (Romans 9:6).

But what I have just said about the Jewish people still being loved by God even if they reject Jesus—while difficult to receive—is easier than the other part of God's covenant with Jewish Israel: the land.

Some say that Jesus never referred to it, and Paul never mentioned it. By this, they mean that while the land was obviously significant for the Old Testament, it is entirely insignificant for the New Testament. There the sole focus is on the whole world, not the little land of Israel.

For many years I agreed with this. But once I started seeing a future for the Jewish people—as Jews—in God's purposes, I also started to see that a future for the land of Israel was also on the radar of the New Testament authors.

But why did I and so many others miss this?

I submit that we have missed the *ongoing* significance of the land in the New Testament because we have been *trained* to miss it. We have accepted the myth that the Old Testament is concerned, after its first eleven chapters, solely with a particular people and a particular land, but that the New Testament reverses that narrow and provincial focus with a new concern for the universal, the whole world. And Paul seems to have confirmed this when he wrote in Romans 4:13 of the promise to Abraham that he would inherit the *world*.

Another reason we Christians have missed the land in the New Testament is that we have missed the overwhelming focus on land in the *Old* Testament. Most of us know that a dominant theme in the Old Testament, perhaps the predominant theme, is covenant. But few recognize that 70 percent of the time, when covenant is mentioned in the Hebrew Bible, it is linked explicitly to the promise of the land. It is also because of the sheer profusion of references in the Old Testament to the promised land: it appears more than one thousand times. According to the *Dictionary of Biblical Imagery,* "longing for land" appears more frequently in the Old Testament than anything else except God Himself. This is particularly so in the Pentateuch. Gerhard von Rad wrote a half century ago, "Of all the promises made to the patriarchs it was that of the land that was the most prominent and decisive."[109]

A further reason that we have lost the theological meaning of the land is that we tend to *assume* that it is not significant anymore, and this assumption has caused us to miss the places where the New Testament suggests that it still is. For example, when Jesus implicitly promised that he would restore the Kingdom to Israel (Acts 1:6), he also told the disciples that the Father "appointed times and seasons by his own authority" for things such as this (Acts 1:7, paraphrase). Scholars have observed that the Greek words for "times" and "restore" are from the same roots (*kairos* and *apokathistemi*) that are used in Acts 3:21 when Peter speaks of future restoration and in Luke 21 where Jesus speaks of the "times of the Gentiles" between the destruction of Jerusalem and its restoration.

---

[109] Gerhard von Rad, *The Problem of the Hexateuch and Other Essays*, trans. E. W. Trueman Dicken (London: Oliver & Boyd, 1966), 79.

This adds weight to the interpretation that in Acts 1:6, Jesus is speaking indeed of a future restoration of Israel in Jerusalem.

The Oxford historian Marcus Bockmuehl has written that this remarkable statement by Jesus shows that the early church expected a future restoration of Israel. I have already mentioned the place where Jesus spoke of the day when the inhabitants of Jerusalem will welcome him (Luke 13:35), and that Paul wrote in Romans 11:29 that the "gifts" of God to Israel were irrevocable. For Hellenistic Jews such as Philo, Josephus, and Ezekiel the Tragedian, the primary "gift" of God to Israel was the land. It is the primary referent for "gift" in all the Old Testament, and arguably for Paul too. Robert Wilken writes in *The Land Called Holy* that early Christians interpreted these and other passages (such as the angel telling Mary that God would give Jesus "the throne of David" and that Jesus would rule "over the house of Jacob forever") as indications of future "restoration and the establishment of a kingdom in Jerusalem." Besides, Paul *did* write of the land in his sermon to the synagogue in Pisidian Antioch. Recounting the exodus, he said, "After destroying seven nations in the land of Canaan, *God gave them their land as an inheritance*" (Acts 13:19, emphasis added). That is covenantal language frequently found in Deuteronomy, where the land is a principal gift of God's covenant with Abraham.

Were these early Christians naive to think that Jesus had any concern for Israel as a distinct land anymore? Didn't Jesus make it clear in his beatitudes that his focus was on the whole earth and not the land of Israel—"Blessed are the meek, for they shall inherit the earth" (Matthew 5:5)? Probably not. More and more scholars are recognizing that a better translation of this verse is "Blessed are the meek, for they shall inherit the *land*." Matthew was translating into Greek Psalm 37:11, where the Hebrew *erets* refers to the land of Israel. In fact, four other verses in Psalm 37 repeat the phrase "inherit the land," with the clear meaning of the land of Israel. The implication was that Jesus' disciples would be able to enjoy the land of Israel (if not live there) in the *palingenesia* or "renewal of all things" that Jesus predicted (Matthew 19:28).

As I have alluded, Peter also seemed to look forward to a special future for the land of Israel. In his second speech in Jerusalem after the Pentecost miracle, he spoke of a future *apokatastasis* or restoration that was to come (Acts 3:21). This was the Greek word used in the Septuagint—which Peter was probably familiar with—for the future return of Jews from all over the world to the land of Israel to reestablish a Jewish nation. Apparently, Peter did not think that the return of the Babylonian exiles at the end of the sixth century BC fulfilled all the prophecies of a future worldwide return to the land.

The author of the book of Revelation was another witness to a future for the land. He wrote that the two witnesses will be killed in Jerusalem (11:8) and the battle of Armageddon will be in a valley in northern Israel (16:16). The renewed earth comes down not as the New Rome or New Alexandria, but as the new Jerusalem (21:2). Its twelve gates are inscribed with the names of the twelve *tribes* of the sons of Israel (21:12), whose mention reminds readers of their life and work in the *land*.

But what about Paul in Romans 4:13? Abraham inherits the world, not just a little land. Doesn't this mean that Christ has overturned any *biblical* right for Jews to possess even part of the land? Not really. First, the context in this fourth chapter of Romans is the Old Testament promises of descendants—people rather than land. Paul goes on in the passage to talk about Abraham being the father of many *nations*. Second, as New Testament scholar Tom Schreiner has pointed out, it was commonplace in Second Temple Judaism (e.g., the Book of Jubilees) to talk about Israel inheriting both the land of Israel *and* the world. The idea was that Abraham's seed would rule the world but also inherit the land of Israel. Not either–or but both–and. This is strongly implied in the Pentateuch, both particularity in the land and universality in blessing to the world. After all, God told Abraham in Genesis 12 that he would give *a land* to the patriarch, and that through him all the families of the *earth* would be blessed (v. 3). This is the same pattern as in Romans 4:13: Abraham would influence the world through his descendants and their land.

Some might concede everything I have written so far but point to John's gospel, perhaps the latest piece of New Testament literature, for evidence that the last major New Testament theologian relativized all these local references to Israel. After all, they would argue, Jesus told the Judeans that his *body* would be the new temple (John 2:21) and informed the Samaritan woman that true worship was no longer restricted to Jerusalem but would now be anywhere as long as it was "in spirit and truth" (4:21–23).

But the formidable New Testament scholar Richard Hays is not so sure that this new worship completely eclipses worship in Jerusalem. In *Reading Backwards* he notes that in Mark's account, Jesus quotes Isaiah's prediction that the temple will become "a house of prayer for all the nations" (Mark 11:17; Isaiah 56:7). This means, for Hays, that Jesus agrees with Isaiah's prediction of "an eschatologically restored Jerusalem" where foreigners will come to God's holy mountain to join "the outcasts of Israel" whom God has "gathered" there. Hays does not think that Jesus' claim about his body as the new temple is supersessionist—as if the Church has replaced Israel—or that this claim is "hostile to continuity with Israel." I would add that, according to Matthew, Jesus believed that God still "dwells in" the temple (23:21). In other words, we can think of the temple in two ways, both as God's house *and* as a symbol of the way that Jesus' body would be God's house. True worship in the eschaton will be in every place where there is worship "in spirit and truth," *and* in the end of days, it will be centered in Jerusalem. The two witnesses will lie dead there (Revelation 11:8); the 144,000 (all Jews!) will stand there on Mt. Zion (Revelation 7:4; 14:1); Gog and Magog will surround the saints there (Revelation 20:9); and the new earth will be centered there (Revelation 21:10; 11:2).

So, there is significant evidence after all that the land of Israel is theologically significant for the authors of the New Testament, not just because of its past history but also because of its ongoing role in the history of redemption. This, of course, begs the question of 1948: Was the establishment of the State of Israel a part of that prophesied history? Is this part of what Jeremiah, Ezekiel, and other prophets meant by their predictions that Jews would return to the land from all over the world? Does this mean that the massive ingathering of Jews to the land in the nineteenth century and then their organization of a protective state are somehow part of the fulfillment of not only Old Testament prophecies but also apostolic expectation of a time of *palingenesia* and *apokatastasis* (renewal and restoration)?

Many Christians do not want to go that far. They are willing to say that God is committed to the *people* of Israel but are wary of connecting their modern return to biblical expectations. They fear that this might suggest a lack of sympathy for Palestinian suffering or Palestinian claims for their own state. Some are willing to say that 1948 might represent God's providential concern for his covenanted people, but that the establishment of the State of Israel falls short of the fulfillment of biblical prophecy.

My response is several-fold. First, there is no reason why Christians cannot support legitimate Palestinian aspirations for justice and statehood and, at the same time, see the establishment of the Jewish polity as a partial fulfillment of biblical prophecy. The Israeli leadership has offered a two-state solution several times to Palestinian leadership—in 1947, in 2000 under Barak, and in 2008 under Olmert. It does not matter what we think of the justice or sincerity of those offers. What matters is that the Jewish state itself has committed itself publicly to Palestinian statehood, so that even the Zionist state does not see its claims for itself to preclude Palestinian self-rule. Neither should Christians think that an eschatological understanding of 1948 precludes Palestinian rights to land and statehood.

But is the Jewish people's political consolidation in 1948 merely a sign of God's providential protection of this people and not an instance of prophetic fulfillment? The present state has resulted from a massive ingathering of Jews from all over the world in the last two centuries. There have always been Jews living in the land—for more than three thousand years—but this recent return was unprecedented. In an uncanny way, it matches the predictions of Israel's prophets *and* the expectations of the New Testament authors. Why is it so difficult to say that the one is connected to the other?

The concern for Palestinians is the answer for some. But as I have just indicated, we non-Palestinian Christians can care for our Palestinian brothers and sisters without denying prophetic fulfillment (at least in part) to the recent return of Jews to the land. Other Christian observers deny fulfillment because of continuing problems and injustices in Israel today. There are injustices large and small experienced by Palestinians, racial tensions, attacks on messianic Jews, government corruption, and what seems to be secularism in many sectors of the populace. These problems seem to make it impossible to say that today's Israel is related to biblical Israel.

We need to recall what we Christians say about ourselves and the church. We are the body of Christ, we say, despite our deep divisions, moral sin, and theological heresies. With all of our egregious spots and wrinkles, we say that we are still a people of God, *prophesied* throughout the Old Testament. In other words, we exercise prophetic and eschatological charity about *ourselves*. Why do we find it so difficult to do the same for another people who are called specially chosen by both Testaments?

Will this be bad for Palestinians? Will it encourage the wrong kind of exceptionalism that would prevent Palestinians from ever having their own state on the West Bank? As I have said, there is no theological reason for thinking so. In fact, the Bible's theological exceptionalism for Israel *requires* that Jews "do righteousness and justice" (Genesis 18:19). Nothing in the promises to Israel precludes their sharing the land with Palestinians. Furthermore, there is biblical precedent for this with Lot (Genesis 13:1–11). Abraham shared the land with Lot.

But going beyond sharing land is living together in peace. Can Palestinians and Jews live together in a way that ensures peace and prosperity for Palestinians? That is already happening to a great degree in Israel proper. But to go further, and especially to bring prosperity and security to Palestinians on the West Bank, it requires asking some hard questions. For example, where else in the Middle East (except in Israel proper) can Palestinians openly criticize the government and sleep securely in their beds? Where else can Arab Christians freely practice their faith?

Those of us in the New Christian Zionism do not take an uncritical approach to the Israeli government. But we also know that Palestinian Christians have more to deal with than just Israelis. They live under a Palestinian Authority (PA) president in the sixteenth year of a four-year term whose regime leaves Palestinian citizens in a climate of fear. They can neither vote nor criticize the PA. In 2017 there was instituted a new cybercrime law that threatens with arrest anyone whose posts on social media are interpreted as criticizing the government. The PA imprisons journalists for exposing its corruption. So, the PA is without accountability.

In 2019 a Palestinian poll found that 61 percent of Palestinians wanted President Abbas to resign. They know that while he and his sons and cronies are profiting enormously from the status quo, most ordinary Palestinians are not. According to Palestinian scholar Kalil Shikaki, 42 percent of Palestinians still want a negotiated settlement toward a two-state solution. But Abbas has repeatedly refused negotiations.

Arab Christians are also threatened by Muslims in the land. When I walked the land of Galilee in 2009, staying at night with both Jews and Palestinians, time and again, I was told by Arab Christians in whispers, for fear of being overheard, "We have our problems with the government of Israel. But our biggest enemy is not the Israeli government but our Muslim cousins and their frightening theology."

Samir Qumsieh, a Christian in Bet Sahour near Bethlehem, fights for the rights of Arab Christians. He has dared to speak out against the subjugation of Christians under Hamas in Gaza. For this, he regularly receives death threats. Once, he was the target of a petrol bomb attack. He says, "Every day we hear and see some radical Muslim cleric speak strongly against Christians. One said recently that Christian Copts should be slaughtered like sheep."[110]

I hope this book will signal to the world that the Israeli government is not the real enemy of the Palestinian people. As long as that is the only message being heard, the real concerns of the Palestinian people are being ignored. I also heard on my walking tour from many Palestinians that they are willing to make peace with Israel, but their leaders are not. Some Palestinians are even willing to concede that God has a plan for both Jews and Arabs in the land. Let's pray that by God's Spirit, hearts will be softened, and minds opened, among both Jews and Arabs, to God's plan for His peoples and land.

## ABOUT THE AUTHOR

Gerald McDermott is the retired Chair of Anglican Divinity at Beeson Divinity School. He is the author, coauthor, or editor of twenty-three books, including *Israel Matters* (Brazos), *The New Christian Zionism* (Inter-Varsity Press), and *Understanding the Jewish Roots of Christianity* (Lexham Press). This chapter is adapted from a speech he gave at a "Christ at the Checkpoint" conference in Oklahoma City in 2018.

---

[110] "Palestinians: The Nightmare of Christians," https://www.gatestoneinstitute.org/9634/palestinian-christians.

*Chapter Thirteen*

# RETHINKING FAITH, ISRAEL, AND THE SOCIAL JUSTICE MOVEMENT

by

**Amy Zewe**

## SOCIAL JUSTICE GROUPS THAT DEMONIZE ISRAEL

Many young Christians entering college life or the working world have a sincere and earnest desire to do good, be good, and express tolerance and compassion, inclusiveness, and diversity. This altruism is noble, and it allows them not only to feel good about themselves but to be accepted by the people around them. The question is: Can you sincerely rally for a cause and not abandon your Christian faith? This examination is designed to help you determine and analyze how your faith and your critical thinking skills can be your biggest asset in helping the oppressed. Who are the groups that people want to help? In the forefront of American and European mindsets surrounding social justice issues, there are several identity groups, including the following:

- African Americans and Black Africans
- Women
- Members of the LBGTQ community

- Palestinians and Arabs (mostly Muslim but some Christians) living in and around Israel, including Gaza and the Palestinian Authority (PA)-controlled West Bank (Judea and Samaria)

What is alarming and a key issue in this examination is that many of the organizations that seek to help these identities vilify Israel in the process. Interestingly, Israel is the only state in the Middle East where the social groups mentioned above live equally and without oppression or fear.

Jews in Israel come in every color of the human skin-tone spectrum—from blond-haired and blue-eyed to olive-skinned, brown-skinned, and black-skinned. Their geographical regions of origin are also quite diverse. During the East African genocide, Israel courageously airlifted tens of thousands of African Jews out of persecution in that region of the world. These Africans were smuggled out of Africa and into Israel, where they were integrated into society. Their children now are at the age of serving in the IDF and attending university. These families enjoy living in a democracy with freedom and access to education, medical care, and freedom to practice their religion. If you are looking for a good movie that accurately depicts one of these rescue missions, watch *The Red Sea Diving Resort* on Netflix. You will be informed, enlightened, and entertained.

## A FACT-FINDING TRIP TO ISRAEL

When I was in Israel on a fact-finding mission in 2008, I met personally with Christians (and others) fleeing from Darfur. Women with children, separated from their husbands, were forced into labor or prison, or even murdered. Many fled murderous gangs with nothing but the clothes on their backs and the children they could carry. These women somehow made it across Africa through Egypt (where persecution was nearly as bad as it was at home) to be met at the borders of Israel with open arms. Scared that yet another armed soldier would abuse them, they were taken to safe and clean barracks, fed, and helped. These women were given care to recover physically and training to learn a skill so they could continue to immigrate to other nations (if desired) to find work and refuge. Many stayed in Israel. Israeli organizations aided in locating husbands, and some were reunited. These people were all black and mostly Christian, but some Muslim. All were assisted with genuine care by Israelis.

In Israel, the color of one's skin, one's religion (remember, Jews, Muslims, Druze, and Christians all live in Israel), and one's gender are met with no systemic or institutional discrimination. Moreover, the atmosphere among Israelis is one of refreshing acceptance.

Women in Israel enjoy the greatest freedoms of anywhere on earth—even rivaling many Western nations. No nation surrounding Israel (and specifically Muslim nations) have the protections for and the access available to women to follow their dreams. Women in Israel of any color, religion, or creed can access the education system through the terminal degree level. Women can serve even in the most forward positions with the IDF. Women are legally protected. Women serve in all levels of government and politics. Women in Israel, even in the so-called disputed territories of Judea and Samaria, work for Israeli companies and enjoy the most worker-centered employment laws in the entire region. More women than men are enrolled in PhD programs in Israeli universities (and not just Jews, but Arabs too).

Members of the LGBTQ community are free to express themselves and live as they please without fear of personal injury or persecution from the government or otherwise. This is impossible within any of the neighboring nations to Israel. Tel Aviv hosts an annual Pride parade that rivals any found in the West. If this were attempted in Egypt, Syria, Lebanon, Jordan, Iraq, or Iran, participants would likely be tortured or executed.

The Palestinian people and issues concerning them are front and center on many US, Canadian, and European college campuses. The term Palestinian is unique, and only about 40 years old in terms of how it is applied and used today. Prior to that, those in the region who were not Jews were called Arabs, and most are and were Muslim, but about 10–15 percent are also Christian. Many Palestinians do not have a good quality of life under Arab rule. Life in Gaza is difficult. Life in the PA is a bit better. Life in the refugee camps in Lebanon or Jordan is horrible. But the history of how they got there, and the current conditions under which they live is not well-known or examined by most, and truth is hidden by the activists claiming to be for their cause. Incidentally, many of today's so-called Palestinians are in their origin Jordanian or Lebanese. Prior to 1948, anyone living in the land identified as Palestine (it was not a nation or a state, but a region) was called Palestinian—including the Jews already there. Interestingly, prior to the granting of statehood to Israel in 1948, the Jewish newspaper in Tel Aviv was called the *Palestinian Press*. An entire generation of Arabs has been raised to call themselves Palestinian and believe they had a state at one time and that they are a nationality. Unfortunately, this is not the case.

## ISRAEL'S EXISTENTIAL BALANCE OF SECURITY AND HUMANITARIAN AID

Contrary to what is reported by the media, Israel is one of the greatest humanitarian benefactors to its Arab neighbors. Gaza receives its electricity, water, medical supplies, and grain from Israel. Arab residents in the PA (West Bank), when surveyed and interviewed off the record overwhelmingly say they would rather have Israeli passports than PA passports and would rather live under Israeli leadership and laws. They would also rather work for Israeli companies because of better pay, better working conditions, better upward mobility, and better quality of life. The women and Christians among the Arab sectors suffer greatly under PA and Gazan leadership. Gazans who protest against their own leadership are persecuted, and Arab journalists are forbidden to report on conditions and sentiments. Israel provides a great amount of humanitarian aid to a region that is consistently attacking the Israeli civilian population. The existential balance of security and humanitarian aid is Israel's constant dilemma.

## WHY ARE THERE PALESTINIAN REFUGEE CAMPS?

When Jews were expelled from Iraq, Iran, Egypt, and North Africa, Israel, a new nation, welcomed them all in and assimilated them into their society. The same was true for the European Jews who fled to Israel before and after the Holocaust. When the Arab League nations told the Arabs in the region to flee their homes before their offensive, now called Israel's 1948 War of Independence, Arabs were told to flee so that Arab armies could commit mass genocide of the Jewish population. Those Arabs that followed the directive were forced into refugee camps that still exist today. For example, in Jordan, approximately 96,000 people have been in the Edom refugee camp for decades. Many are of Jordanian origin, but Jordan does not allow them to assimilate into their society—no schools, no work, etc. The same case exists in Lebanon as well. Palestinians—Arabs who share the same culture, religion, and language—are not accepted or assimilated into the neighboring nations, causing great suffering. The Palestinian leaders have historically exploited the suffering of their people to draw world opinion against Israel and raise billions of dollars to support their own lavish lifestyles.

I bring these few issues to your attention because these are some of the most popular social justice platforms: minorities, women, LGBTQ, and Palestinians. However, many of today's popular mainstream social justice organizations claiming to support these causes do so while falsely blaming and demonizing Israel. One can only assume the motivation is driven by antisemitism.

## SOCIAL JUSTICE MOVEMENTS AND CORRUPTION

Organizations that are raising money, support, and awareness for social justice causes include Black Lives Matter, the Women's March, and Students for Justice in Palestine (SJP). Those of you on social media or on college campuses (or both) can likely name other organizations that rally for different causes. It's important to vet these organizations by reading their agendas and manifestos. To call for justice for one group by erasing justice for another is not justice but injustice. Many social justice groups have submitted to the concept of intersectionality. This concept allows groups with polar opposite goals to find commonality with one another because of the shared interest of social justice. For example, LGBTQ organizations stand in solidarity with radical Islamic groups seeking social justice. What is amazing about this is Islam calls for the murder of lesbian and gay people. How is the marriage of these two groups even possible? Intersectionality. The trend in the most popular social justice groups today is their commitment to a false narrative that demonizes Israel. A frightening thread woven through many of the groups bound together by intersectionality is an antisemitism so violent it calls for the mass genocide of all Jews living in the land of Israel today.

## A CHALLENGE TOWARD CRITICAL THINKING AND REMEMBRANCE

My plea to you is this: Guard your God-given quest for justice and compassion and your burden to help others from being hijacked or leveraged by the often antisemitic agendas in many of the social justice organizations today. As Christians, we must recognize the place God has in His plan for Jews as a people and Israel as a nation. As you examine the causes that touch your heart and realize your compassion for others who are oppressed, you cannot solve a problem without fully defining it and knowing its history. That is where your bright minds and critical thinking skills can come in handy. Do not believe what others tell you about a problem or a solution. Find out for yourself. Armed with some basic historical facts and not allowing others to stereotype you (or bully you), you can contribute to society for causes you believe in without compromising your integrity and without unwittingly entering into antisemitic agendas that seek to lift up one group by brutalizing the Jewish people.

May we never forget the alarming truth that Hitler led a social justice movement known as the Nazi National Socialist Workers Party that sought justice for German Aryans while blaming the Jews for all of Germany's social and economic problems. Antisemitic Nazi propaganda flourished on German college campuses and ultimately unleashed multitudes of angry young baptized German Christians who abandoned their faith and became Hitler's willing executioners of six million Jewish men, women, and children—all under the guise of social justice.

## ABOUT THE AUTHOR

Amy Zewe is the CEO of the business consulting firm Alseata, Inc. She is an adjunct university professor of business communications and humanities courses. Amy is the vice-president of The Jerusalem Connection International and generates weekly video blogs called "Red Alerts," focusing on BDS, antisemitism, and Anti-Zionism. Amy has participated in two study tours of Israel and completed her master's thesis on human rights in the modern State of Israel. Amy holds a master's degree in humanities with an emphasis on political philosophy from Tiffin University. She also holds a graduate degree in professional writing from the George Washington University and undergraduate degrees from Azusa Pacific University and Columbia Bible College and Seminary (Bodenseehof, Germany campus).

*Chapter Fourteen*

# A CALL FOR YOUNG WOMEN TO STAND WITH THE JEWISH PEOPLE

**by**

**Carrie Elise Simms**

A hero's heart and character are formed in the crucible of suffering in order to produce a foundation of empathy, compassion, and courage, which is repeatedly tested in crisis and self-sacrifice. In his book *Leaders Eat Last*, Simon Sinek notes:

> Leaders are the ones who run headfirst into the unknown. They rush toward the danger. They put their own interests aside to protect us or to pull us into the future. Leaders would sooner sacrifice what is theirs to save what is ours. And they would never sacrifice what is ours to save what is theirs. This is what it means to be a leader. It means they choose to go first into danger, headfirst toward the unknown.

Today, in the face of growing antisemitism, the world is in desperate need of young women to boldly enter the political arena. Heroes choose courage no matter the cost to themselves personally. Indifference has been edited from their vocabulary. Holocaust survivor Elie Wiesel wisely counsels, "The opposite of love is not hate, it's indifference. The opposite of art is not ugliness, it's indifference. The opposite of faith is not heresy, it's indifference. And the opposite of life is not death, it's indifference."

Elie Wiesel was a Romanian-born American Nobel Laureate, writer, professor, political activist, and Holocaust survivor. He authored fifty-seven books, including *Night*, a work based on his experiences as a Jewish prisoner in the Auschwitz and Buchenwald concentration camps.

Elie personally experienced injustice. His mother and sister were murdered at Auschwitz, and his father was beaten to death in Buchenwald. Miraculously, he survived and eventually immigrated to the United States. Elie wrote extensively about his personal and painful experience during the Holocaust and states:

It is obvious that the war which Hitler and his accomplices waged was a war not only against Jewish men, women, and children, but also against Jewish religion, Jewish culture, Jewish tradition, therefore Jewish memory. . . . We cannot indefinitely avoid depressing subject matter, particularly if it is true, and in the subsequent quarter century the world has had to hear a story it would have preferred not to hear—the story of how a cultured people turned to genocide, and how the rest of the world, also composed of cultured people, remained silent in the face of genocide.

Orphaned in her childhood like Elie Wiesel, Hadassah (Esther in the book of Esther in the Bible) understood the pain and grief of loss at an early age. Also like many Jews in Europe during the Holocaust, Hadassah hid her identity, becoming Esther, Queen of Persia. For over 2,500 years, we have celebrated the heroism of Esther during the festival of Purim (a Jewish feast that celebrates God's deliverance from their planned extermination at the hands of Haman, a leader in the Persian

Empire). Esther was the Wonder Woman of her generation who skillfully and successfully conquered injustice and a political genocidal plot.

How is Esther's story relevant today?

Several years ago, I was selected to participate in a Biblical Discipleship Conference based on vocation. Every vocation was divided into ten categories or domains. Our domain consisted of individuals working in the military, government, and politics. At the beginning of the week, every participant was asked the following three questions:

1. What is the unique culture within your vocation? Also, describe it in order to enable individuals outside your domain to better understand you and your vocation.

2. Are there biblical examples of individuals who served in your vocation?

3. How would you like other domains to see your vocation and biblical examples differently?

Each domain processed these questions individually and collectively. We interacted with the other participants throughout the conference as well. At the beginning of the week-long discipleship journey, several pastors asked me why I was at the conference. They shared their belief that it was unbiblical for Christians to serve in the political arena. At the end of the week, each domain selected a representative to present our findings to all of the domains represented at the conference. I was selected by my group to share our answers with the larger body. I prayed for wisdom and courage as I stood before hundreds of Christian leaders to reveal our collective response. Our group responses to the three questions are as follows:

1. In the domain of government and politics, we often serve with and for narcissistic individuals. Consequently, we have learned to navigate very challenging individuals who often sacrifice us in order to succeed. Therefore, we do not trust easily. In our

suffering, we have embraced how to overcome offense, and we have learned obedience to God and God alone.

2. A majority of the biblical heroes of our faith served in the military, government, and political positions for the preservation of God's people, including Moses, David, Joseph, Daniel, Joshua, Samuel, Deborah, Nehemiah, Mordecai, and Esther. The Messiah will defeat and overthrow an anti-Israel Global Leader, and rule and reign in Jerusalem. It will be the greatest political coup in world history.

3. Many Christian leaders have misrepresented the political mission of the Heroes of our Faith, stripping their lives of their political roles throughout Scripture. For example, Christian sermons and movies depict Esther as a beautiful, naive young lady who won a beauty pageant and became a modern-day Miss America or Cinderella. This view devalues her incredible courage, character, and the very complex and political context of her life and heroism.

Conversely, the Jewish perspective accurately understands Esther was the first lobbyist in Scripture, a political operative, an intelligent and courageous woman. She successfully exposed the enemy of the Jews, tried and executed Haman and his entire family, and secured new competent political leadership to write and enact legislation, which delivered every Jew from annihilation in the vast Persian Empire. Every year, Esther is celebrated for her faith, courage, intelligence, and political victory during Purim. Holocaust survivors understand the importance of engaging in politics. Again, in the wise words of Elie Wiesel: "There may be times when we are powerless to prevent injustice, but there must never be a time when we fail to protest."

Christian leaders who believe Christians should *not* be involved in politics misrepresent Scripture and the heroes of our faith. More heroes of our faith were placed in critical and strategic political positions than all of the other vocations combined throughout the Bible.

Their political mission was motivated by faith, not fear, courage, not cowardice, obedience, not opportunism, commitment, not compromise, and purity, not pride.

Political leaders determine all of the rules and regulations that impact every vocation. The absence of godly men and women in Congress affects every school, ministry, church, synagogue, business, hospital, community, and arena in America. If godly individuals avoid involvement in this political domain, our nation suffers the consequences.

Some contend that biblical faith has no place in the political process. It is their belief our nation would enjoy greater freedom if it were liberated from the laws of God and our national motto: "In God we trust." Is a belief in God detrimental or beneficial to the public policies of a nation? Should the values of women and men of faith be tolerated in America? Throughout history, women and men, *because of their faith*, positively influenced the public policies of their nation. Almost 2,500 years ago, King Xerxes reigned over a vast empire from India to Ethiopia. His chief advisor, Haman, motivated by his contempt for the faith of one man, Mordecai, a Jew, set in motion a decree of antisemitic genocide, which could not be revoked according to Persian law. He created legislation that would annihilate every Jew in Persia because he determined they were a detriment to the kingdom. If it were not for the faith and courage of one woman, Esther, the Jews of Persia would have ceased to exist.

> Then Haman said to King Ahasuerus, There is a certain people scattered abroad and dispersed among the peoples in all the provinces of your kingdom; their laws are different from every other people, neither do they keep the king's laws. Therefore, it is not for the king's profit to tolerate them. If it pleases the king, let it be decreed that they be destroyed, and I will pay 10,000 talents of silver into the hands of those who have charge of the king's business, that it may be brought into the king's treasuries. (Esther 3:8–9)

As women enter the world of politics, our primary commitment must be to God and God alone. As we walk in obedience, the Lord will enable us to navigate the maze of political correctness and provide the wisdom and courage required to stand against individuals that do not support Judeo-Christian values. Many Christian leaders genuinely believe it is unbiblical to enter into the political arena. What does the Bible actually teach us? In Esther chapter 4, Mordecai (Esther's uncle) asked Esther to lobby the king to revoke Haman's legislation (decree) to annihilate every Jew throughout the vast Persian Empire. Esther initially responded in fear:

> All the king's servants and the people of the king's provinces know that any person, be it man or woman, who shall go into the inner court to the king without being called shall be put to death; there is but one law for him, except [him] to whom the king shall hold out the golden scepter, that he may live. But I have not been called to come to the king for these thirty days. (Esther 4:1)

Here is Mordecai's brilliant response:

> Do not flatter yourself that you shall escape in the king's palace any more than all the other Jews. For if you keep silent at this time, relief and deliverance shall arise for the Jews from else-where, but you and your father's house will perish. And who knows but that you have come to the kingdom for such a time as this and for this very occasion? (Esther 4:13–14)

At first, Esther refused to get involved because she was afraid she might lose her life. Mordecai directly addressed her fear, stating she would actually lose her life if she remained silent. Thankfully, Esther overcame her fear and recognized God had placed her in a politically strategic position to save the lives of her people. Her obedience, courage, political valor, and love for her people overcame her fear and indifference. Esther saved the life of every Jew in Persia.

We must overcome our fearful indifference and obey God no matter the cost to us personally. As antisemitism is on the rise in America and around the world, the choice of fear or faith is before you. Choose faith and courage. Do not remain silent. We each have been placed in critical positions of influence in our synagogues, churches, communities, and families *for such a time as this*! Here are more wise words from Holocaust survivor Elie Wiesel, taken from his speech upon receiving the Nobel Peace Prize in 1986:

> I swore never to be silent whenever and wherever human beings endure suffering and humiliation. We must always take sides. Neutrality helps the oppressor, never the victim. Silence encourages the tormentor, never the tormented.

If you are a woman, you are called to be an Esther. You were created to be wise, strong, political, biblical, and noble. I implore you to evaluate your position on the issue of Israel. Is it based on a love for God and His people, the Jewish Community? Perhaps you have been called to the kingdom for such a time as this—to be an Esther in your generation, willing to stand against antisemitism.

> *Our lives no longer belong to us alone; they belong to all those who need us desperately. . . . To remain silent and indifferent is the greatest sin of all.*

> **—Elie Wiesel**

## ABOUT THE AUTHOR

Carrie Elise Simms is the vice president and chief operating officer for the Advanced Security Training Institute (ASTI). ASTI's mission is to ensure the safety and security of American citizens. ASTI's School Safety, Counter Terrorism, and Cyber Security Israel Immersion Training Course provides critical training and education for US members of Congress and US first responders. ASTI showcases Israeli experts in the security field who share their knowledge and vast experience with US leaders to better protect American citizens. Simms is the founder of For Such a Time as This, which focuses on building relationships between American and Israeli leaders. Simms served on the Board of Directors of Toward Tradition, an Orthodox Jewish organization, which expanded her knowledge and understanding of Jewish history and culture.

*Chapter Fifteen*

# A CALL FOR YOUNG MEN TO STAND WITH THE JEWISH PEOPLE

### by
### Dexter Van Zile

It's pretty incongruous for a fifty-five-year-old Catholic from Boston to put the call out to young evangelicals and ask them to become pastors, teachers, and worship leaders in their respective churches and spark a spirit- and Bible-based revival in the United States, but that's what I'm doing. We need a twenty-first-century Billy Graham, or more accurately, a whole bunch of twenty-first-century Billy Grahams, to lay the groundwork for a full-blown religious revival in the United States, because if it does not happen, we are headed for disaster.

Your mission, should you choose to accept it, is to engage the hearts and minds of young people, young men especially, and bring them into the fold of a robust and resilient Christian faith that gives them a fighting chance to become a blessing to the people around them despite the challenges they and their country will face in the years ahead. Your mission will not be easy.

You will be in competition with a growing number of wolves in sheep's clothing who use the internet to transform troubled young men living in vulnerable solitude into a mob of haters who blame the Jews for every setback they and their country endure.

These wolves in sheep's clothing will be your dread opponents, as will be the folks who sell opioids on the street or pornography on the internet. Your job will be to protect, immerse, and restore lives threatened by these and other addictions with the word, body, blood, and water of Christ Himself. To do these things, you, too, will have to immerse yourself in the life and suffering of Christ through prayer, reading, and action.

It is a demanding and consequential call, but your friends are in trouble, and they need your help. They, like you, are struggling to cross the stream onto the far shore of responsible adulthood. It's your job to help those young men cross that stream free of the crippling millstone of antisemitism tied to their ankles.

I realized just how much trouble America was in early April 2019. I had written two articles about Owen Benjamin, a failed actor and stand-up comic who had taken to YouTube to spew hatred toward Jews from his farm in the state of Washington. Benjamin, who had an unhappy childhood (for which he blames his father) while growing up in upstate New York, had fled to Washington after his brief acting career in Hollywood came to an end. Once in Washington, Benjamin became a professional antisemite, a preacher of hate, soliciting donations during nightly livestreams he posted on YouTube. Using his webcam to connect to his viewers, Benjamin said hateful things about Jews, describing them, for instance, as "a tribe of people that goes from dog to dog just getting blood." He was generating real money for his rants. When he was finally kicked off YouTube for violating its terms of service, the company sent him his last check for $30,000. That's real money.

I was a bit late to the game in responding to Benjamin's rants. Dr. Michael Brown, author of *Our Hands Are Stained with Blood*, which recounts the tragic relationship between the church and the Jewish people, had already produced a video that highlighted some of the more hateful things Benjamin had said. Predictably a bunch of antisemitic trolls had started to leave ugly comments underneath Dr. Brown's video. In light of the hateful comments, I felt obligated to come to Dr. Brown's defense with two articles of my own, both published in *The Times of Israel*. Benjamin responded with disdain, posting an image of one of my articles on the screen while he made fun of my last name, substituting "Vile" for "Zile." (I can't tell you how many times I've heard that one.)

I was glad to get under his skin, but I was bothered by the possibility that I may have helped Benjamin increase his audience by condemning his rants. For sure, I hadn't hindered him any. Within a few days, after my articles were published, Benjamin went from having 246,000 followers to 253,000 subscribers on YouTube. Rooting around on the internet, I discovered that in March 2019, Benjamin displayed an image from his YouTube account that indicated his viewers in the United States had watched more than forty-nine million minutes' worth of his videos in the previous twenty-eight days.

That's a lot of views for a guy who described Jews as "the most racist people on the planet who think that they can rape you, lie to you, and steal from you without any ramifications because they think they are genetically chosen when they're not." It's a lot of exposure for a guy who declared that because of their evil mindset, "Jews end up being in charge of the most disgusting industries, pornography, opioids, war, media, and Hollywood." Eventually, Benjamin was kicked off YouTube and Twitter and prohibited from soliciting donations on PayPal and Patreon. He moved onto other venues, and people kept sending him money.

Clearly, there was a demand for Benjamin's Jew-hatred, and he was not the only one who was meeting it. E. Michael Jones, a historian who had been fired from his first job as a history professor at St. Mary's, a Catholic college in Indiana, and had generated a following of Jew-haters of his own, was a regular guest on Benjamin's podcasts. A prolific author of antisemitic tomes that he sold via the internet, Jones provided an aura of theological and intellectual sophistication whenever he appeared on Benjamin's livestream.

Speaking at a conference in Tehran in February 2013, during which he portrayed Jews as having a corrupt influence on American society, Jones declared, "Iran is the leader of the free world." He also described the shootings of Jews at synagogues in Pittsburgh, Pennsylvania, and Poway, California, as a response to the role "the Jews" have played in undermining the moral order. The Christian moral order, Jones said, has been "overridden by an operating system or by software that you would call 'The Jews.'"

"They've been undermining the moral law in the name of liberation," he said. "That's what abortion is. That's what pornography is. That's what gay rights is. And now, that's what Zionism is." Jones is particularly adept at connecting the difficulties young men face in their lives, such as addiction to pornography, to the Jews. The first part of his message is, "Don't watch porn," which is a laudable and necessary exhortation young men need to hear. But then he goes onto say pornography is a Jewish conspiracy to undermine Western manhood. He ties a message of masculine restoration to Jew-hatred. We have seen that before.

If we look closely at those moments in history when antisemitism gets the most traction, they are marked by a crisis in masculine identity. France struggled with a rise in antisemitism in the decades after it suffered a humiliating loss in the Franco-Prussian War in 1870. It culminated in the Dreyfus Affair when Alfred Dreyfus, a French Jew, was wrongly convicted of spying for Germany in 1895. The humiliated men who led France and its army, who were still suffering the aftereffects of their loss to Germany in 1870, found their scapegoat twenty-five years later. The folks who persecuted Dreyfus were trying, in part, to restore their dignity at the expense of an innocent Jew. Eventually, Dreyfus was freed and exonerated, but not without a huge controversy that divided the country for more than a decade.

A similar, but much more lethal, process of wounded masculinity expressing itself as antisemitism took place in Germany after that country's devastating loss in World War I. When Hitler came along and preached his hateful message about the Jews to the men who served in the war and to the young men who grew up in the shadow of Germany's defeat, he had a ready-built audience. He turned these young men into killers, started a war that cost sixty million people their lives, and created a bureaucracy that murdered thirteen million people, including six million Jews in Eastern Europe.

We have a similar cohort of young men in the United States who are vulnerable to the siren call of Jew-hatred. You know the men I am talking about. We have seen them on television duking it out in the streets of Portland, Oregon, and in Charlottesville, Virginia. Angry young white men from both the left and right, folks from Antifa and the white supremacists, who oppose one another ideologically and politically but have one thing in common: rage. They aren't mad; they are volcanically angry.

The prospects of being able to start a career, get married, buy a home, and raise a family are at an all-time low in the United States, particularly in light of the COVID-19 crisis, which prompted officials throughout the US to enact policies that cost millions of people their jobs. Under these circumstances, it's no surprise that synagogues are regularly threatened and vandalized and sometimes attacked by gunmen who write manifestos that include ideas popularized by the men I've written about.

The fact is, we are now confronted with a subculture of Jew-haters who can recruit supporters into their ranks via the internet, which is used to normalize Jew-hatred and the violence it inspires. They use the internet the same way Hitler used the microphone and radio broadcasts to connect to a mass audience. Getting these folks banned from YouTube, Twitter, and Facebook might help in the short term, but not forever, because people are drawn to the forbidden. We need to find a way to inoculate people against these ideas. Preventing their exposure to them is impossible. Somebody needs to get to their target audience of angry young men first, or at least soon enough in their emotional, intellectual, and spiritual development to prevent them from embracing the millstone of hate offered to them by these purveyors of hatred.

That's where you, dear reader, enter my narrative. I'm not asking you to be the next Dietrich Bonhoeffer, the great Protestant theologian who is invoked by everyone and his mother as the great anti-Nazi preacher of the twentieth century. It may be heresy to say so, but the fact is, when it came to gathering disciples and followers to their respective causes, Hitler did a better job recruiting followers than Bonhoeffer. What Germany needed was not a Bonhoeffer who pointed out how folks were betraying Christ, but a Billy Graham figure who could help follow in Christ's path. Every young man that Hitler recruited to his cause was a follower that Christian pastors—Bohnoeffer included—had failed to bring into the fold of Christ. These men had emotional and spiritual wounds that the church was simply unable to balm. Men were brought back from the war, but not brought into the fold. Nominally, they may have been Christians, but there was nothing about their lived experience as Christians that protected them from Hitler's appeal.

As antisemitism grows in its appeal to young men in your generation, what message can you offer them? The same one Paul the Apostle offered—following Christ in His suffering. The challenge you present to your audience will be a simple one. They must choose between joining their suffering with the redemptive wounds of Christ or embracing the hatred of Christ's Jewish brethren fomenting from the microphones of modern-day Jew-haters looking for a scapegoat for their own pain and suffering. Antisemites offer one alternative. You must enunciate—and embody—the other alternative for your sake and the sake of the people you love and for the sake of Christ's Jewish brethren and for the sake of Christ Himself.

## ABOUT THE AUTHOR

Dexter Van Zile is a Shillman Research Fellow for the Committee for Accuracy in Middle East Reporting and Analysis (CAMERA). His work is focused on anti-Israel propaganda broadcast by Christian churches and parachurch institutions and the failure of Christian peace activists to address human rights abuses in Muslim-majority countries in the Middle East. He has played a major role in countering misinformation broadcast into Christian churches by Palestinian Christians and refuting antisemitic propaganda broadcast by white nationalists and their allies in the US. His articles have appeared in *The Jerusalem Post*, *The Boston Globe*, *Jewish Political Studies Review*, *The Algemeiner*, and *The Jewish News Syndicate* (JNS).